T5-BPY-843

# THE HOLY GRAIL AND THE SHROUD OF CHRIST

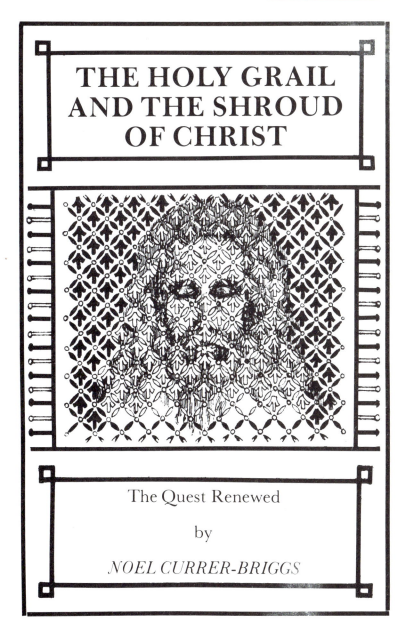

The Quest Renewed

by

*NOEL CURRER-BRIGGS*

BT
587
.54
C87
1984

Copyright © 1984 Noel Currer-Briggs
First published 1984
by ARA Publications, 25 Harrow Piece, Maulden, Beds. MK45 2DG


All rights reserved. No part of this publication may be reproduced,
stored in a retrieval system, or transmitted, in any form or by any
means, electronic, mechanical, photocopying, recording or
otherwise, without the prior permission in writing of ARA
Publications.

ISBN 0 9509468 0 X

Design and artwork by Michael Myers M.S.I.A.D.
Cover design based on the Laon Icon.
Phototypeset by Performance Typesetting, Milton Keynes.
Printed in Great Britain by Andus Print, Luton.

# CONTENTS

# ACKNOWLEDGEMENTS

WITHOUT THE UNSTINTED help of Ian Wilson and Dr Eugen Csocsán de Várallja, the greater part of this book would not have been possible. They have afforded me the very greatest assistance and their criticism has been beyond price. It has been the misfortune of my many friends to have been obliged to put up with endless chatter about Grails and Shrouds; David Reynolds and Audrey Summerskill have read one version of the book and corrected endless mistakes and pointed out glaring omissions and contradictions. Jack Iles and Reu Sloman had to sit patiently while I read it to them aloud one wet Sunday afternoon and were then kind enough to point out obscurities in it. They also lent me their house for several months so that I could do research at Cambridge. Patricia Hamilton and Rena Beech typed large sections of it, unravelling my dreadful handwriting with a skill beyond praise.

In the course of writing this book I have been greatly helped by Dr Marc Heine, Dr Alexis Vlasto, Robin Cormack, Professor Bernard Hamilton, Susan Black, Madame Suzanne Martinet, Madame Margaret Audin, Maître and Madame Boudriot, Uwe Siemon-Netto, all of whom have placed their time and knowledge at my disposal. I am also endebted to Editions "Mage" for permission to include a reproduction of the icon of Laon as a frontispiece to the Salesians of Don Bosco for leave to publish photographs of the Shroud of Turin, and to Michael Myers for designing the cover and drawing the maps and other help he gave me in the design and preparation of the book. I would also like to thank Royston Gambier for drawing up the genealogical tables and Anne-Marie Ehrlich for picture research. Mark Le Fanu has likewise been of great help and encouragement to me with advice about publishing one's own work.

I am also deeply grateful to Jacques de Brabant who gave me his opinion on the French sections of the book, and also to the staffs of the Archives Départementales of Côte d'Or, Hérault and Dordogne who went to great trouble to seek out obscure works and documents for me to consult. I must likewise thank Abel Branchu for lending me his copy of Christian Bernadac's book on Otto Rahn which opened my eyes to the strange goings-on of this Nazi writer. Without the help of John Buchanan-Brown I would have wasted much time before coming upon vital evidence concerning the Templars.

Finally, I have to thank those many friends who in the course of two years have put me up and put up with me. To all of them I dedicate this book.

Verteillac, Dordogne 1982–1983

# FOREWORD

SEVEN YEARS AGO, in the preface to my own book attempting to reconstruct the Turin Shroud's early history, I wrote:
"Undoubtedly future writers will correct and modify some of the more pioneering conclusions drawn . . ." It was a genuine hope for the future, occasioned by my own uncertainties on many problems surrounding the Shroud's origins, not least being the obscure period between the disappearance of the cloth of Edessa (with which I identified the Shroud) from Constantinople in 1204, and the first reasonably certain emergence of the Shroud proper in the possession of the French de Charny family during the 1350s.

Initially, despite the intense public interest raised by the Shroud expositions in 1978, it seemed as if few scholars were prepared to venture their insights into a field most regarded as still far too precarious. Such caution was not shared, however, by Hungarian-born Oxford scholar Dr. Eugene Csoscán de Várallja, who wrote to me not long after my book's publication with a graphic new hypothesis of the Shroud's likely adventures in the immediate wake of the Crusader sack of Constantinople in 1204. For the first time, I learned the haunting and colourful story of Hungarian-born princess Mary-Margaret, married to the middle-aged Emperor of Constantinople while still a girl of ten, flung into obscurity due to her husband's overthrow in an internal coup, restored to her rank by a Crusader rescue mission, cast aside again, widowed in the course of the Crusader sack of Constantinople, re-elevated by a whirlwind marriage to a leader of the Crusader forces, widowed again, only to marry for a third time, into a family closely associated with the Order of Knights Templar. As rightly recognized by Dr. Csocsán de Várallja, here was a woman who would have been particularly close to the Shroud if it was one and the same as the Mandylion of Edessa. And not a few clues seemed to suggest that she had taken the Shroud with her to the place to which she moved after leaving Constantinople: Thessalonica where she rededicated a church to the cloth "not-made-by-hands", and Sirmium where would seem to have been painted the Shroud/Mandylion copy known as the "Holy Face of Laon". Most telling of all was Mary-Margaret's subsequent association with the Order of Knight's Templar, with whom I had identified much of the Shroud's "missing years".

But the story was still loose-ended. How did the Shroud get from the Templars to the de Charnys? Who were the de Charnys, that they could acquire such a theoretically fabulous relic? The genealogical problem posed in my book, whether there was a family relationship between a Templar Geoffrey de Charnay and the first indisputably Shroud-owning Geoffrey de Charny, remained unresolved. Then, amidst the world-wide correspondence my book continued to generate, came an enthusiastic letter from noted genealogist Noel Currer-Briggs, who unknown to me had been making his own researches into some of the very same questions. In the interests of furtherance of human knowledge I put Noel Currer-Briggs and Dr. Csocsán de Várallja in touch with each other, and so this book was born . . .

As becomes realised by anyone who embarks on the Shroud as a topic of research, it is one riven by controversy and dissension, even among upholders of the cloth's authenticity, and it would be wrong to infer that I necessarily support all this book's arguments, particularly those relating to Montségur. But as one of Britain's most well-respected genealogists, Noel Currer-Briggs has made a particularly valuable and thought provoking contribution to Shroud studies. He has chosen to do so, furthermore, in an especially pivotal year, for at the time of writing there are high hopes that it may be this very autumn that the Shroud will be radiocarbon dated for the very first time . . .

Ian Wilson

February 1984

# PART ONE
## *The Holy Grail Identified*

# ONE

THE LETTER ASKING me to take part in a new quest for King Arthur reached me in August. There was a lot of work being done in France, it said, and someone was needed to act as a liaison between the English author, who spoke no French, and the French scholars who spoke no English. As this was the kind of invitation I can never resist, I eagerly accepted it. I had no idea then that it would lead me to a solution of a mystery which has confounded scholars for more than seven hundred years.

August in the Dordogne, where I was then living, was hotter than usual that year. The crowds of tourists were also bigger than I liked. Ribérac market resounded on Friday mornings to the ecstatic cries of folk from Esher and Huddersfield rather than to the more usual chatter of peasants from Verteillac or Tocane. It would be cooler in the Pyrenees, I thought, so why not take a few days off and go to Montségur in search of the Holy Grail? I had just finished a book which tried to make out that the Grail was not a relic at all but the holy blood line, the Sang Real, of Jesus. This highly controversial theory had caused something of a stir in England – the French, of course, just roared with laughter – and I thought it might be fun to see if I could do any better. I had to admit that I, too, found it difficult to take, not because the idea of a married Jesus in any way shocked me, quite the contrary, but because the authors seemed to have jumped to some fairly way-out conclusions, although I had to admire their diligence and the depth of their research.

1

I could accept that Jesus, being an orthodox Jew and a Rabbi had probably been married. The fact that the gospels have nothing to say about this didn't trouble me unduly. His wife might indeed have been Mary Magdalene, and for all anyone knew, they might have had a quiver-full of children. But I did find it hard to believe that these might have been the ancestors of the Merovingian kings of France, and this was a matter of some relevance, for these self-same Merovingians were the contemporaries of King Arthur, so the theory seemed to me to leave a good deal to be desired. From these kings many noble and royal families descend to the present day, and the blood line of the Merovingians, stemming from Jesus and Mary Magdalene would, if it could be proved, be a good deal bluer than most. If the authors of this book were to be believed, the Holy Grail was not the Chalice of the Last Supper, as most of us think, but the true blood of Christ, the holy Y-chromosome, as it were. The mysterious Cathar treasure, stored away for so long in the castle of Montségur was, in other words, none other than the knowledge of this secret, which had been passed down from generation to generation, through Isaac Newton, Jean Cocteau and Claude Debussy (to name but a few). In brief, the stuff of which best-sellers and popular TV programmes are made.

Although I couldn't agree with the authors' conclusions, I felt that there might be something in what they had to say. Anyway I had never been to Montségur, so why not take a trip down there to see what I could find? I am a great believer in the theory that places reveal as much to the researcher as documents. To get the lie of the land can be immensely helpful in making up one's mind about events that happened there. And so I set out for the south. On may way I began to speculate about the origin of the word "Grail". Why did this object which had been the inspiration of so much romantic literature come to be called a Grail? What did the word really mean? I knew that Geoffrey of Monmouth made no mention of it in his account of King Arthur, and that none of the earliest Arthurian legends before the first part of the twelfth century did either. I wondered when the word first appeared and in what language. Years ago as a student I had read Wolfram von Eschenbach's *Parzival*, the German legend upon which Wagner based his operas "Lohengrin" and "Parsifal". I remembered that Wolfram had based his version on an earlier French one by Chrétien de Troyes, but I could not recall in what respect they differed from each other or from other early anonymous versions and that of Robert de Boron.

The holy blood-line theory claimed that Montségur was the site of Wolfram's Grail castle Munsalvaesche; could this be proved, I asked myself, or was it just an inspired guess? Wolfram claimed to have had knowledge which Chrétien lacked; this, the authors alleged was none other than the secret of Jesus' marriage and family. But was it? The fundamental mystery seemed to me to lie in the many apparently irreconcilable and contradictory descriptions of the object itself. If the Grail was so intimately associated with Jesus, and if, indeed, it ever existed, why were there no references to it of any kind before the twelfth century? Where was it all this time? Why did it not figure in earlier literature, folklore and tradition? Why should something of such deep religious significance be hidden for so long?

The pre-Christian Celtic foundation underlying the Grail romances has been thoroughly explored, and most commentators agree that they are rooted in pagan antiquity. At the same time, from the middle of the twelfth century this pagan substructure underwent a complete transformation; the Grail became uniquely linked with Christ's Passion and with King Arthur and his knights. These romances became the sci-fi epics of their day, flourishing for over a century from about 1190 to 1300. In time they became almost a cult of their own, in spite of their being somewhat unorthodox from a strictly Christian and ecclesiastical point of view. In 1470 the theme reappeared in England with the publication of Malory's "Morte d'Arthur", and continues to fascinate people to the present day.

Some students of the Grail romances suggest that they were deliberately written with the intention of mystifying the reader; that the aim was to conceal something so sacred and secret that only the initiated could find it. It is certainly a good idea to disguise what you want to hide in such a way that those who are bent on finding it look for something quite different. Was it possible that this had happened in the case of the

Grail? Did those who actually owned it – always supposing it was a relic that really existed – deliberately seek to put people off the track in order to protect it? Who might they be protecting it from? The Church? The State? common or garden thieves? I realised that I was by no means the first to ask such questions, but before I could give any answers I would have to find out why the object was called the Grail, who gave it that name and when. Until I had solved this fundamental problem, it would be pointless to pursue the matter any further. Guesswork was not good enough; I had to construct a hypothesis based on the etymology of the word itself, and perhaps on other words associated with the Grail, and then try to disprove it. It is easy enough to advance a theory and then to produce evidence to support it; my theory had to be disproved by such evidence as I might find. Having discovered how the relic got its name would, I hoped, indicate at once whether it had ever existed or not. If it had, then I could begin to look for something which had a history of its own outside the confines of romance. How all this might help to establish the historicity of King Arthur was something else altogether. If he had lived at all, it was some six hundred years before the Grail appeared in the legends associated with his name. If both were the figment of the troubadours' and chroniclers' imagination, then my particular quest had ended before it had begun. I could not believe that. The evidence for the historicity of Arthur is overwhelming; my task was to prove the historicity of the Grail, and to explain why it became grafted on to the legends of the great British hero. Of one thing I could be certain. These legends would not have had the enduring popularity they have enjoyed for so long if they had appeared to be pure fiction to those who first read them. The medieval courts of the twelfth and thirteen centuries were made up of highly educated and well-travelled men and women. They took to these stories because they struck at the heart of their own lives and experience. They were not ephemera to be briefly enjoyed and then forgotten.

   The more I thought about it the more I felt the answer must lie in the religious and political history of the twelfth and thirteenth centuries. This was the age of the Crusades and of the Knights Templar; modern research on the Shroud of Turin had pointed to a possible link with the Templars and the Grail legends; literary commentators see in the Knights of the Round Table a romanticized version of the Knights Templar. Was the Shroud the missing link in the chain? or could the basic mystery arise from more prosaic causes such as linguistic misinterpretations, clerical errors, even, perhaps, deliberate falsifications? If the Shroud were a truly ancient artefact and not a medieval forgery, where was it before it came to light in Champagne in the 1350s? Who were its owners at that time and what was their ancestry? If, as Ian Wilson, the leading authority on the history of the Shroud, believes the Shroud is identical with a relic known to have existed in Constantinople from the middle of the tenth century until the beginning of the thirteenth, where was it during the time before it re-appeared in France? Who owned it then? Wilson suggests it may have belonged to the Templars, and I knew that that order had been founded by men from Champagne. If the Grail and the Shroud were in some way connected, could this explain why it had been so hard to identify? If one or both these objects had belonged to the Templars could they have had a vested interest in making people look for the wrong object in the wrong place? By 1470, when Malory wrote his *"Morte d'Arthur"*, the Grail had assumed a more distinct identity as the Cup of the Last Supper. This did not explain why there had been at least nine other identities.

In one account, the Grail is a vessel containing a single wafer. This could be a small plate or a cup. In another it is large enough to dispense both food and drink to a large company of knights. Yet another account describes it as the receptacle for a severed head. Several versions call it a dish or platter made of gold and encrusted with jewels. Another calls it simply a bleeding head. Wolfram von Eschenbach describes it as a kind of magic stone as well as a series of changing images of Christ. Modern commentators have seen in the ceremonies attendant upon the appearance of the Grail, reflections of the Byzantine Mass.

Before I could claim to have solved the mystery of the Holy Grail I would have to find an object which would reconcile all these conflicting decsriptions. Until I solved the fundamental problem – namely the origin of the word itself – I would be no more successful than countless of my predecessors.

If you look up "Grail" in any encyclopaedia, you will find that the origin of the word is said to be uncertain. You will next be told that it probably comes from the Low Latin word "Gradalis" or "Gradalus" meaning a shallow vessel. On the other hand some dictionaries suggest that it derives from a lost word "Cratale" deriving from the classical Latin word "Cratus" which ultimately comes from the Greek "Crater", from which our modern word crater, as in volcanoes, is derived. The Latin Cratus means a chalice, cup or goblet. So here we are, back where we began. I feel instinctively mistrustful of lost words. How can a word get lost? Surely the lexicographer who wrote this was guessing how Grail might have derived from Cratus, and in order to make his case convincing has had to invent a "lost" word. When I explored other dictionaries I found that in Languedoc the word "grazal" means a large clay vessel; in Provençal "grasal" signifies a bowl or platter; in Anglo-Norman "graal" is said to mean a dish made of some costly material for the purpose of great feasts. Once more, I had to ask myself, how much of this was guesswork with the benefit of hindsight? These words occur in the legends of the Holy Grail, and so the lexicographers have attributed their meanings in the light of the descriptions I have just given above. It is rather as though some investigator in the thirtieth century set out to discover the origin of the term "Rolls". He would easily find out that it was applied in the twentieth century to a type of motorcar and to a razor. This would not help him very much until he found out *why* this word was applied to two such different objects. One dictionary might explain that the car was so called because it rolled along so smoothly, but this would not help to explain how the razor got its name. Only when he found out that E.S. Rolls had been a brilliant engineer who built superb motorcars, and that in the course of time the name "Rolls" came to signify an article of outstanding craftsmanship, might he guess that a particular type of razor had been given the name Rolls to indicate its excellence. And so it is with the Grail – a grail is a grail is a grail – not very helpful.

In one of the early versions of the legend, known as the

*"Perlesvaus"*, written anonymously between 1206 and 1212, perhaps by a Templar, the Grail is described in the following terms:-

> 'Two maidens come out of the chapel, one of them carries the Grail in her two hands and the other the Holy Lance, which still carries traces of blood on it. They walk side by side and come into the room where Sir Gawain is eating. A sweet odour pervades the room. Sir Gawain looks on the Grail and it seems to him there is a - - - - - within it.'

And here confusion occurs, for one version says that the Grail contained 'une chandoile' (a candle) and another says 'un calice' (a chalice). This is a very important point. Gawain 'seems' to see either a candle or a chalice *within* the Grail. It is made clear that whatever Gawain saw, it was within and not on the Grail. Now if the Grail were a chalice, it would be nonsense to place another chalice within it. On the other hand, the word 'chandoile' if used symbolically, makes more sense, for it can be taken to imply some kind of radiance. But the text is more explicit, for it goes on to say,

> 'donc il n'est gaires a icel tens'

which means

> 'albeit there was none at that time.'

so the whole sentence should read

> 'Sir Gawain looks on the Grail and it seems to him there is a candle (or radiance) within it albeit there was none at that time.'

This suggests that what Gawain saw was not literally a candle, but a sense of light or radiance such as many believers say they experience when seeing a particularly holy relic for the first time. The following passage, indeed, supports the view that this is intended symbolically, for Gawain 'seems' to behold two angels carrying a golden candelabra with lighted candles, after he has seen the Lance from which the blood flows. The French text uses the words 'senble' and 'voit' deliberately to indicate what Gawain actually sees and what he seems to see.

A little later in the story the two maidens come out of a second chapel. This time Gawain 'seems' to behold three angels, where before he had beheld only two. He also 'seems' to behold *in the midst* of the Grail the form of a child. Once again, we are faced with the problem of explaining how the form of a child could fit into the midst of a chalice. It just doesn't make any sense.

The third vision of Gawain is similar to the other two insofar as the writer makes a distinction between what Gawain sees and what he seems to see. Once again the two maidens come before a table, but Gawain seems to see three. He looks up and there appears before him a man nailed to a cross with a spear fixed in his side. The maidens return to the chapel and take away the Holy Grail and the Lance. The knights leave the table and go into another hall leaving Gawain alone. The vision-like quality of this episode is emphasised by the recurring motif of three drops of blood which Gawain sees after the form of the child. He cannot take his eyes from them 'and would fain pick them up but they elude him . . . wherefore he is very doleful, for he cannot put his hand out to them nor anything within his reach.'

Wolfram von Eschenbach claimed to have had privileged information as I have already said. He wrote between 1200 and 1216, and quotes an earlier account of the legend written by Chrétien de Troyes some dozen or so years before, which he says was incorrect. Wolfram says that the Grail is not an object of fantasy, but a means of hiding something of great consequence. In a passage in which the knight Parsifal meets his hermit uncle, Trevrizent, the latter describes the Grail as follows:

'It is well known to me that many formidable fighting men dwell at Munsalvaesche with the Gral. They are continually riding out on sorties in quest of adventure. Whether these same Templars (Wolfram uses the term "Templeisen") reap trouble or renown, they bear it for their sins. A warlike company lives there. I will tell you how they are nourished. They live from a stone whose essence is pure . . . It is called *Lapis exilis*. By virtue of this stone the Phoenix is burned to ashes, in which she is reborn. Thus does the Phoenix moult her feathers. Which done, she shines dazzling bright and as lovely as before . . . Such powers does the Stone confer on mortal men that their flesh and bones are soon made young again. This Stone is called the Gral. The Gral is unknown, save to those who are singled out by name to join the Company of Munsalvaesche.'

As I drew closer to the Pyrenees my excitement increased. I had recently read that extraordinary book "Kreuzzug gegen den Graal" (The Crusade against the Grail) by the Nazi, Otto Rahn, who had done more than anyone else to identify Montségur and the surrounding district of Ariège with Wolfram's Munsalvaesche. I knew that Rahn had influenced Rudolf Steiner and the Theosophists, and that there were many followers of this faith who still came from France, Holland and America to seek solace in these mountains at the feet of gurus from California and the Far East. Wherever a mystery exists there are always those who have their own subjective and comforting solutions. No group of people and few places have suffered more from this process than the Cathars and Montségur. Certainly no visitor to this part of France can fail to be impressed by its grandeur and beauty, by the romantic remains of its mountain-top castles, by its vast caverns and deep gorges. The Ariège is one of those places which stimulate the imagination and lend themselves to the telling of stories and the weaving of myths. And because of the horrors they suffered and the basic tolerance of their faith, the Cathars have still much to offer those who today are looking for a new religion and for consolation in their unhappiness. Above all, these mountains, like the Himalayas, have become for some a Shangri-La in which they hope to find new hope and comfort. It is no coincidence that the greatest centre of orthodox pilgrimage in Europe should be at Lourdes among these splendid peaks and valleys.

I think it is a mistake to dismiss all this out of hand; it cannot all be fantasy and subjective nonsense. At the end of the day I find myself unable to accept the bulk of the theories concerning the Cathars and their treasure, but I cannot totally reject the possibility that Montségur may have been the inspiration for Munsalvaesche, and that the castle itself may have housed an important relic of some kind. That is not to say that it was any of the relics I shall be considering in this book, but as my search proceeded I was driven more to the conclusion that if the treasure were not the Grail itself, then it may have had something to do with it.

It was very early in the morning when I first came to Montségur. I had spent the previous night at Quillan, and set out before eight o'clock to avoid the crowds of tourists who flock to the place at this time of year. It was one of those days when the first autumn mists were still shrouding the tops of the mountains, and when I parked my car at the foot of the peak on which the castle is built I had to pick my way upwards through a damp fog. As I neared the summit, the castle walls rose up out of the murky vapour, but only when I was less than fifty yards away from them and some feet below. The place was deserted as I walked around the walls and climbed the rough flight of steps leading to the ramparts. Looking outwards I could see nothing but swirling cloud, and within the enclosure it was hard to see the remains of the keep at the other end. It was a ghostly experience, and I found no difficulty in understanding why the imagination of countless visitors has been stirred throughout the castle's long history.

As I got into the car to drive away the clouds parted and looking upward, some thousand feet above me, the castle emerged like a great grey battleship from a smokescreen. No Wagnerian set-designer could have done anything half so romantic. I got out of the car again and walked back across the field to the small stone memorial erected to commemorate the death of the Cathar victims of that holocaust seven hundred and forty years ago, and began to understand how people's lives can be changed by such as this. On my way home to the Dordogne my mind was full of what I had just witnessed, of the tragic history of the place and the character of the Cathars who went to their death so bravely in defence beliefs not so very different from those I had been brought up with myself, for Unitarianism traces its origins to the Arian heresy of the Visigoths from whom the people of Languedoc are descended.

Why, I kept asking myself, why was the sacred object called "The Grail"? How did it become associated with King Arthur and GlastonburyWhat possible connection could there be between this stupendous, savage mountain scenery and the Cathar heretics who lived here, and the lush, peaceful meadows of Somerset? How could a sixth-century British chieftain have the remotest connection with a group of thirteenth century heretics, let alone with Richard Wagner and the crazy philosophy of Hitler? The only common factor was the Grail, and this did not help much, until I could uncover its true identity.

And so, when I got home, I started my quest for the Holy Grail in the pages of Chambers Encyclopaedia, the Oxford English Dictionary, Larousse, the Glossarium Mediae et Infimae Latinitatis, the Dictionnaire d'ancien Français and as many others as I could get hold of. Munsalvaesche – Montségur: the notion of safety, security, salvation . . . Could it be that Wolfram had, indeed, chosen the name from a personal knowledge of Montségur? Otto Rahn thought so. He believed that Wolfram had travelled through the Ariège on his way to Spain, and there is nothing inherently improbable in that. The troubadours and minnesingers travelled the length and breadth of Europe, and the Court of Aragon was renowned for its patronage of them. Some commentators suggest that Munsalvaesche and Terre de Salvaesche derive from the French 'sauvage' or 'salvage'. These words derive from the root 'silvaticus', which means wild woodland. That is certainly a possibility. But it is equally likely that the term derives from 'salvare', to save. Words deriving from the Latin 'salus/securitas' have subtly different but linked meanings. The former have come to suggest a spiritual condition of safety or wholeness; the latter a freedom from danger – something wholly physical. The sheer strength and apparent impregnability of Montségur is certainly impressive. Perhaps the choice of Munsalvaesche was deliberate in order to convey the idea of the spirituality of the Grail it was supposed to house, yet at the same time to hint at a secure fortress which may have really existed.

It all boils down to this: no one can say where Munsalvaesche was beyond the fact that it was several days journey from Nantes in a mountainous region and was not separated from Waleis, the land of Parsifal's birth, by water. The Pyrenees are the nearest mountains to Nantes, but if Waleis is Wales, as most commentators would have us believe, then somehow we have to get rid of the English and Bristol channels. This difficulty has led others to identify Waleis with the Valais (German Wallis) in Switzerland, but since this name derives from the word meaning valley, it could apply to a host of places. Geoffrey Ashe and Jessie Weston, two of the most eminent Arthurian scholars, tend to discount the identification of Montségur with Munsalvaesche because Parsifal is connected with Anjou and Wolfram does not mention the Pyrenees specifically. Professor Hatto, on the other hand, makes it plain that a study of the journeys of Parsifal and Gawain show that Wolfram did have a coherent map of both real and unreal places in his mind. Personal and place names, not only in Wolfram but throughout the legends have caused a great deal of debate. The names of real people and places are interspersed with fictitious ones. In Wolfram, for instance, Nantes, Rouen and Toledo are mentioned alongside Cucumerlant, Schanpfanzun and Gippones. No one should be surprised at this, for it has been the custom of writers from Virgil to Agatha Christie and beyond to mix made-up names with real ones in order to lend credence to their stories. When it comes to people, considerable efforts have been made to identify the characters with ones from real life. Lohengrin, for example, was never Duke of Brabant any more than Killirjacac was Count of Champagne. The holders of these titles in Wolfram's day were called Henry and Theobald.

By now it must be clear that puns, double meanings, hidden meanings and the exploration of dictionaries and glossaries had a large part to play in the solution of the mystery. The two punning derivations of Munsalvaesche are equally appropriate when applied to Montségur, which is both wild, savage, and a place of holiness to which countless pilgrims once flocked to seek their salvation, and it is also surrounded by forests. As I went deeper into the matter I realized that nothing was quite what it seemed on the surface, but that every name and every circumstance had its own deeper significance.

Munsalvaesche is not the only name given to the castle of the Holy Grail. Another version of the legend written down between 1215 and 1235 a decade or so after Wolfram's, is known as the "Great Vulgate Cycle'. There is considerable controversy over the authorship of this work, and I was soon to discover that this led me into some unexpected fields of research. Not the least of these debates concerns the language in which it was first written. As we have it today, the language is medieval French and the Grail Castle is called Corbenic. This word appears to be derived from the words 'cors' and 'beneiz' or 'beneit'. 'Cors' can be translated in at least six different ways: corner, horn, court, course, heart and body. 'Beneiz/beneit' on the other hand, is generally taken to mean blessed or holy. The words 'cors beneiz', meaning literally holy body, are often used to indicate the body of Christ or Corpus Christi, and in the legends where they occur in association with the words 'saint Graaus' this is invariably so. The Arthurian scholar, R.S. Loomis, put forward a theory that the term referred obliquely to the food-and-drink-providing Horn of Plenty or to the ancient Celtic holy dish of Brân the Blessed. He supports his thesis with many ingenious and scholarly references to pagan literature, and builds a huge structure on a somewhat slender foundation. But Loomis is typical of those who have tried to establish the identity of the Grail and of its mysterious custodians and of their relationship to the blessed body of Christ, either in the sacramental or historic sense.

The origin of the name Corbenic has thus been the subject of much learned debate, which traces it to the improbable Chaldean word for 'Most Holy Vessel' and the equally unlikely Welsh word for corn. The letters 'c' and 't' are constantly being mistaken for each other in medieval manuscripts because they looked very much alike. A Dutch version of the legend calls the castle Cambenoyt and another early French version Corlenot, from both of which the more familiar

Camelot might be derived. Bearing these variants in mind, it does not seem unreasonable to believe that the original name was Corbenoit or Corbeneit. These can be translated therefore as the Castle of the Holy Body (or the Castle of Corpus Christi), the Castle of the Court of the Blessed (or the Castle of the Holy Court), the Castle of the Sacred Heart. Less plausibly it could be the Castle of the Horn (of Plenty). The other two meanings of 'cors' make even less sense. Taken in the context of the legends by far the most likely translation would be the first.

The common factor linking the names Corbenic and Munsalvaesche is that of holiness insofar as salvation and blessedness are religiously connected with each other. In the case of Corbenic, no geographical identification is possible – the name is purely symbolic. I began to wonder why the Grail Castle should have different names in the French and German versions of the legends, and whether there might be any significance in this. At first I could think of none, but gradually as my search progressed, I realized that if Montségur was to be identified with Munsalvaesche, this had to stem from events that took place in 1205 or 1206. These dates fall well within the limits of time during which Wolfram is known to have written *"Parzival"*. If it could be shown that he wrote his poem before 1205, then I could see no way in which Montségur could have been his model. That the term Corbenic was not used until twenty years or so later became increasingly significant, as I hope to show by and by.

# TWO

IT WAS AT THIS POINT in my quest that I began to study the history of the Turin Shroud in the hope of finding the answer to some of these tantalising questions.

Saint Nino, a Georgian princess, visited Jerusalem in the fourth century, and wrote an account which can be found in Wardrop and Conybeare's translation of "Studia Biblica et Ecclesiastica" Volume Five. This shows that the Shroud was still believed to be preserved by the faithful in Jerusalem at that time. In 438, the Empress Eudocia, wife of Theodosius III, also visited Jerusalem. The purpose of her visit was to collect relics for the new church of St Mary Blachernae which she and the Empress Pulcheria were building at Constantinople. Nicephorus Callistus, writing in the early fourteenth century gives from sources now lost a list of relics she sent back. Among these are the "Spargana" of Christ, which some authorities translate as the swaddling clothes, but which can also refer to funerary cloths or bandages. There is, however, no record of any holy swaddling clothes at Constantinople, so it is possible that the term here refers to the Shroud and the other funerary linens such as the bandages which encircled the shroud after the body was placed in the tomb, and those to which St John refers in Chapter XIX: 40 "Then took they the body of Jesus, and wound it in linen clothes with the spices, as the manner of the Jews is to bury", and in XX: 6-2 "Then cometh Simon Peter following him, and went into the sepulchre, and seeth the linen clothes lie, and the napkin, that was about his head, not lying with the linen clothes, but wrapped together in a place by itself." Traces of the napkin or bandages which were bound round the head to support the chin can be seen on the Shroud itself. The frontal and dorsal images of the head appear to be divided rather than contiguous, as one would expect. Scholars believe that this can be explained by the presence of a cloth or bandages which have interposed a layer or layers of cloth between the crown of the head and the Shroud. Assuming that the image was made by the physical contact of the body with the linen, these bandages would have prevented any marking at this point.

There is yet another story told by Adamnan of Iona about 705. A certain Bishop Arculfus was shown at Jerusalem a linen sheet about eight feet in length bearing the figure of Christ on it, which was said to be the actual Shroud, and this is repeated by a French monk, Bernard, in the eleventh century and by Peter the Deacon, a monk of Monte Cassino, in the twelfth. The latter's account, which refer to events in 1140, suggest that this cloth was in Jerusalem at that date. On the other hand, the Shroud was certainly in Constantinople by 1150.

This confuses the issue, for this was the date of the Second Crusade led by King Louis VII of France, in which Constantinople took no part. If so notable a relic had left Jerusalem at this time, it would have gone to France rather than Byzantium. Saint John Damascene (in his De Imaginibus), writing in the eighth century mentions "sindons" among the relics of the Passion, and Saint Braulion of Saragossa, a century earlier, mentions the "linteamina et sudarium quo corpus Domini est involutum" (the linens and shroud in which the body of the Lord was wound).

None of these references help us to decide where the Shroud was kept at that time, but they do at least show that it ranked among the chief relics of the Church.

It is possible that Eudocia removed the real Shroud, which became known as the Mandylion, but left a copy of the frontal image only in the Holy Land, which measured eight feet against the fourteen feet or more of the true Shroud. This is extremely important, as I was to discover, when I came to look into the history of the Besançon Shroud. As so often happened, the copy, in time, came to be taken for the original without any intention to deceive, and helps to explain why there were so many duplicate relics in the Middle Ages which were venerated as genuine.

Ian Wilson makes a case for believing that the Shroud and the miracle-working image of Christ, known as the Mandylion of Edessa (later of Constantinople) are one and the same. He supports his theory by a wealth of historical, scientific and artistic evidence, none of which has been seriously challenged. Without claiming that the Shroud is the authentic cloth in which Jesus was buried, he makes out a convincing case for believing that it reached Constantinople in 945 and disappeared from that city after it was sacked by the Frankish Crusaders and the Venetians in 1204. He traces the history of the Shroud as we know it today from its appearance in Champagne in about 1356 to the present time. This leaves what he calls a "dark period" of some one hundred and fifty years during which, if the two relics are identical, it disappeared. He advances sound historical reasons for believing that it passed into the hands of the Knights Templar at this time. The Templars, as I have already said, were known to have been associated with the emergence of the Grail legends.

The Order of Knights Templar was founded by noblemen from Champagne and Burgundy to defend Christianity against the Saracens at the beginning of the twelfth century. It reached the height of its power and wealth during the thirteenth century and was finally suppressed in 1317. Thus the dark period of the Shroud falls within the period of the Templars' greatest influence, as do the earliest versions of the Grail romances.

The legend of the Mandylion is worth telling at some length because of the light it sheds on certain aspects of the Grail stories. According to the legend as it had developed by the tenth century, Abgar, the Toparch of Edessa and contemporary of Jesus, suffered from leprosy and arthritis. One of his servants, Ananias, happened to be travelling through Palestine on his way to Egypt, when he saw Jesus in the distance performing some miracles. On his return journey Ananias made it his business to find out more about Jesus and his powers of healing. When he got back to Edessa, important city on the upper Euphrates, he told Abgar about the amazing Jewish healer he had seen. Abgar was so impressed he wrote a letter to Jesus asking him to take the trouble to come and heal him, and sent Ananias back to Palestine to deliver it. He told him that if he couldn't persuade Jesus to come to Edessa, he was to bring back a portrait of him so that he might look upon it and be cured.

Ananias went back to Judea and found Jesus preaching to a crowd of people. He sat down as near to him as possible and began drawing Jesus' portrait. Jesus, realising that his portrait was being drawn, sent Thomas to bring the artist to him. Ananias then handed Jesus Abgar's letter, which he read with great care. He then sat down and wrote a reply declining to come to Edessa, but promising to send one of his disciples to cure Abgar. Jesus also promised Abgar and his people eternal life and to provide Edessa with a sure defence against its enemies. Knowing that Ananias had been asked to bring a portrait back with him, Jesus washed his face and dried it on a towel and 'in some divine and inexpressible way' impressed his likeness upon it. He gave the towel to Ananias, telling him to give it to Abgar so that he might be cured.

On the way home Ananias stopped at the city of Hierapolis, where he lodged outside the town for the night at a place where there was a heap of tiles, under which he hid the sacred towel. During the night a great fire broke out which threatened to destroy the city. Ananias was arrested on suspicion of having started it. He was at a loss to explain the cause of the fire, but told the authorities that he had hidden a bundle among the tiles from where the flames had seemed to emanate. The citizens searched the spot at once and found not only Ananias' bundle but also, on one of the tiles nearby, another copy of Jesus' face, which they kept as a relic. They set Ananias free and sent him on his way with the cloth.

After he got back to Edessa, Ananias delivered Jesus' letter and the cloth to Abgar, who was immediately cured. The cloth, continued to keep its miraculous powers and many who looked upon it were cured of their ills. Abgar was baptized and a Christian community was established at Edessa.

The account relates how Abgar 'fastened the cloth to a

board and embellished it with gold, which is now to be seen,'
He put it for safe keeping in a niche above one of the gates of
the city, where it was venerated by all who entered that way.
After a time, however, many of the citizens relapsed into
paganism, but a small remnant of Christians remained. The
bishop of Edessa at that time took the precaution of bricking
up the niche where the cloth was kept, lit a lamp in front of it
and placed a tile over it to protect it from damp, thus concealing it completely.

The cloth remained hidden and forgotten for many
centuries, until Edessa was attacked by the Persians. Then
someone remembered Jesus' promise to protect the city; a
search was made and the cloth was rediscovered. The tile
which had been placed on top of it was found to be engraved
with another likeness of Jesus similar to that on the cloth.

The Persians were defeated and Edessa once more reverted
to Christianity. The Emperor of Constantinople had a great
cathedral built to house the cloth and the tile, and Edessa
became a centre of pilgrimage. Consequently new images 'in
every way like the original, as near perfect a reproduction as
possible, drafting with men's materials as close a resemblance
as they could to something not made by hands', were commissioned and distributed far and wide.

In time Edessa fell under infidel rule, and the Emperor
asked the Edessans to let him have the relics to add to his
collection in Constantinople for safe keeping. The Christians
of Edessa were reluctant to let them go, but the Emir agreed,
and the cloth and the tile were taken away to Constantinople,
where they arrived on August 15, 944. The casket containing
the cloth and Jesus' letter to Abgar were placed in the Pharos
Treasury of the Boukoleon Palace, and the tile, which became
known as the Keramion, was lodged in the church of St Mary
in the Blachernae Palace.

This story is to be found in the official account of the Mandylion commissioned by the Emperor in 945, the year after its
arrival in Byzantium. Although this does not claim that
Abgar's "towel" was the shroud in which Jesus was wrapped
in the tomb, it is now generally thought to refer to the latter,
the story having been modified to calm the sensibilities of
those who might have regarded the shroud as unclean.

Laon Cathedral                    J. Feuillie/© C.N.M.H.S/S.P.A.D.E.M.

Another explanation is attributed to the fact that the cloth was folded in such a way that the author of the account of 945 was unaware that it was a shroud, since only the face was visible.

In 970 the Mandylion was processed in Constantinople, but the cloth was not publicly exhibited or taken out of its casket. It was seen again in 1058 in the cathedral of Saint Sofia. Writing in about 1130, an Anglo-Norman monk, Ordericus Vitalis, in his history of the church, tells the story of Abgar of Edessa and his miraculous cure, and refers to the Mandylion as the shroud of Christ. Since his history was widely read throughout France and England, this is probably the earliest reference to the relic in western Europe, and coincides in time with the publication of Geoffrey of Monmouth's history of the kings of Britain, which includes an account of King Arthur's reign. In 1203, Robert de Clari, a French Crusader, describes a public exhibition of the Shroud/Mandylion at the church of St Mary of Blachernae.

The account of 945 states that copies of the Mandylion in its golden casket were made and sent to churches throughout the Christian world, and several of these have survived to the present day. A much later copy is to be found in the Treasury of the cathedral of Laon in northern France*. This icon was bought by Jacques Pantaléon, then Archdeacon of Laon and later Pope Urban IV, from a convent in Bari in southern Italy, around 1249, for his sister, the abbess of a nearby convent in Picardy. After her death, the icon passed into the possession of the cathedral chapter who still own it.

When you compare the face depicted on the Laon icon with that on the Shroud, there can be little doubt that the artist was making a faithful copy of what he actually saw. In other words, this is no work of imagination. Indeed, the Slavonic inscription he has painted beneath the face more or less says as much. It reads OBRAZ GSPDN NAUBRUSJE (obraz gospodin na ubruzje) which means "The Lord's picture on the cloth." If you look carefully at the bottom of the icon, you can even see what looks like a row of tassles or a fringe such as one might find on a shawl. David and Tamar Talbot-Rice, the leading British authorities on the dating of icons, consider that this one was painted around 1200, and all authorities agree that it was painted in the Balkans.

---

*See frontispiece.

Now, as I shall subsequently describe, one of the places to which the Mandylion may have been taken after it disappeared from Constantinople in 1204 was the abbey of Szavaszentdemeter, then in the Hungarian province of Sirmium, now in Northern Yugoslavia. The eminent Hungarian historian, Eugen Csocsán de Várallja, points out that the Abbot of Szavaszentdemeter acted as bishop to those who adhered to the Byzantine rite in Hungary. The abbey itself was on the north bank of the river Sava near the modern town of Jasenovac, some thirtyfive kilometres west of Bosanska Gradiska and about sixty to the south-east of Zagreb at the point where the river Una joins it. It was not therefore a Serbian monastery, which would have been Orthodox or Byzantine, but it played an important role in the cultural life of Slavonia, which was then a Hungarian province, and which now forms part of northern Yugoslavia. If, therefore, the Laon icon is a direct copy of the Shroud, painted by someone who had seen the Shroud/ Mandylion, from which he may well have copied it, and if as I later discovered, there are good reasons for explaining how the Shroud may have got to Szavaszentdemeter, then it is highly likely that it was painted there. Szavaszentdemeter was the only place of importance in Hungary where Church Slavonic was used. It could not have been painted at Esztergom, the then capital of Hungary, for example, since the language used in churches there was Latin. But we know that the abbey of Szavaszentdemeter was in communion with Rome from at least 1216 until the fall of the Latin Empire of Constantinople in 1261, and there is surviving correspondence between the Popes and the monastery in which the former confirmed its rights and privileges. This covers the period during which the icon and the Shroud/Mandylion must have reached western Europe.

A very similar painting, now badly damaged, is still to be seen in the monastery of Gradac in Central Yugoslavia. These, and examples in Russia and Egypt, are all similar in design and show what had been done with the cloth when Abgar "covered it and embellished it in gold." Jesus' head appears set in a circle or oval on either side of which is a latticework design, making the whole rectangual in shape. It seems clear that the trellis or lattice, which in the case of the Laon icon is all in gold, represented the embellishment that the artists have faithfully copied from the original. The circular "halo", which is to be seen in all these representations, is merely the absence of trelliswork round the face. Because the cloth was folded so that only the face was visible, few people knew that when it was unfolded it revealed the frontal and dorsal image of the body. This dramatic fact was undoubtedly known to the custodians of the Mandylion, who were high ecclesiastical functionaries close to the Emperor and the Patriarch. The whole cloth could not, however, be displayed without a certain amount of dismantling and gadgetry.

In order to achieve this shape, it was only necessary to fold the cloth in half and then in half again, so that the back and all the front (except the face) was hidden. Knowing the size of the Turin Shroud, it is possible to calculate the approximate size of the casket in which the Mandylion was kept. As the Shroud measures 14ft 3in by 3ft 7in, when folded as I have described, the casket must have been under 4ft by 2ft and no deeper than was needed to contain eight thicknesses of linen, say about six inches. Here then, was the key to the mystery. The term lattice or trellis is synonymous with grid or grill, and they all derive from the medieval French word 'greil' or 'greille'. This, in turn derives from the Low Latin words 'craticula' or 'gradella' which both come from the classical Latin word 'cratis'. So we find two Latin words differing by only one letter, both of which could refer to varying descriptions of the Holy Grail. One of these is 'cratus', which becomes 'gradalis' or 'gradalus' and ultimately Graal; the other is 'cratis' which becomes 'gradella' and ultimately 'greil(le)'. No wonder there has been so much confusion.

Before Ian Wilson published his book on the Shroud of Turin in 1978, no one would have dreamt that a word deriving from 'cratis' could possibly have anything to do with the Holy Grail as it is depicted in the romances. But having broken the key to the enigma, I had now to test my theory to see if it deciphered the code. I had to look at the legends in the light of this new information as well as establish what had happened to the Mandylion and Keramion after the sack of Constantinople in 1204. At first I thought that the 'cratis' explanation would fit all the descriptions of the Grail to be found in the earliest legends, but I was driven inexorably to the conclusion that there were some that would not. Was it possible that there were more than one holy object to which the term 'grail' was applied? The answer seems to me to be an undoubted 'Yes'.

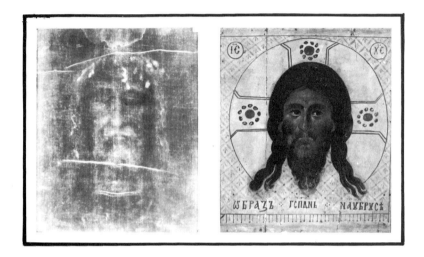

Face of Christ on the Shroud                              Laon Icon

# THREE

HAVING FOUND THE KEY to the cypher, I had now to decode the message. In other words I had to examine the various versions of the legend to see how the descriptions of the Grail fitted my identification of it as the golden latticework casket containing the Shroud.

There are six main groups of legends. The earliest is the *Conte del Graal* attributed to Chrétien de Troyes, a troubadour from Champagne. The second group consists of Robert de Boron's metrical *Joseph of Arimathea, Le Petit Saint Graal*, the *History of Merlin* and what is known as the Didot-Modena *Perceval*. I have already briefly mentioned the Great Vulgate Cycle which is made up of four works, the *Quest of the Holy Grail, Merlin*, the prose *Launcelot* and the *Death of King Arthur*. The fourth is known to scholars as the pseudo-Robert de Boron Cycle and is generally regarded as an alternative version of the Great Vulgate Cycle. Then there is the German cycle consisting of Wolfram's *Parzival*, Albrecht's *Titurel* and the *Diu Crône*. Finally we have the version known as the *Perlesvaus*. To these can be added the Welsh version known as the *Peredur*, which forms part of the ancient collection of stories known as the *Mabinogion*, written down sometime between 1050 and 1250.

I decided to examine these versions, as far as I could, in the order in which they were written. This was not easy, as the date of writing is not a true indication of the date of compilation, for they existed as memorized stories long before they were committed to parchment or paper. In the end I began with the *Peredur*, because being Celtic in origin, I felt it must be the most ancient of the British versions.

The hero, Peredur, the counterpart of Wolfram's Parsifal, visits his uncle and they talk together:

> 'He saw two lads entering the hall and then leaving for a chamber. They carried a spear of incalculable size with three streams of blood running from the socket to the floor . . . After a short silence two girls entered bearing a large platter with a man's head covered with blood on it, and everyone set up a crying and lamentation . . .'

This seems to be a blend of Parsifal's encounter with his uncle Trevrizent, from Wolfram's version and the incident concerning Sir Gawain from the *Perlesvaus* that I quoted in chapter one. Because the date of the *Peredur* is so uncertain, it is hard to say whether the passage I have just quoted was written before or after the existence of the Mandylion became known in Wales. No one seems to be sure whether Ordericus Vitalis' reference to the story of Abgar in his church history of 1130 was the first intimation of its existence or not. It is certainly the earliest written record we have, but it doesn't necessarily follow that no one knew of it before Ordericus set it down in his book. All we can say is that the *Peredur* Grail is of such a size that two girls are needed to carry it, and that it is described as a large platter big enough to carry a man's head.

This fits what we know of the Mandylion casket perfectly. Admittedly this incident has been interpreted as referring to John the Baptist, whose severed head Herodias asked to be given her on a platter. At the same time, if you think of the head of Jesus as seen within its halo-like, trelliswork casket, the description fits admirably. A similar mistake was made not so long ago when the portrait of a bearded man was found on the back of a wooden panel in a cottage in Templecombe in Somerset. This was at first thought to be a medieval picture of John the Baptist until it was shown to be a head of Jesus which had formerly been in the Templar preceptory nearby. I shall have a good deal to say about the Templar's "Head" in due course, but for the present we must continue our examination of the Grail legends.

The *Perlesvaus* Grail, in addition to the changing images I have already described, is likened to a severed head which Sir Gawain sees 'in the midst' of it 'all in flesh'. This struck me as a particularly interesting description, especially when considered in the context of the other passages I have already quoted. You will remember that when the Grail first appeared to Gawain, he seemed to see a radiance within it, then he saw the image of a child and finally a man nailed to a cross with a spear in his side.

Now, it was the custom on Good Friday at the church of St Mary of Blachernae in Constantinople to hold a special mass which lasted all day. According to a twelfth century account of it inserted in a sermon given by the eighth century pope Stephen III, Christ was made to appear 'at the first hour of the day as a child, at the third as a boy, at the sixth as an adolescent and at the ninth hour visible in his full manhood, in which the Son of God went to his Passion when he bore for our sins the suffering of the Cross.'

Robert de Clari, whom I mentioned briefly in the last chapter, left a vivid eye-witness account of the Fourth Crusade, which culminated in the sack of Constantinople in April 1204. He has this to say of the church of St Mary of Blachernae:

> '(Here) was kept the sydoine in which Our Lord had been wrapped, which stood up straight every Good Friday so that the features of Our Lord could be plainly seen there.'

He also said that the 'sydoine', or shroud, was preserved there in a 'dish'. It seems to me that Gawain's vision, the historical account of Pope Stephen's sermon and Robert de Clari's account of the Blachernae Mass must all refer to the same ceremony. All three seem to show that the Shroud was unfolded bit by bit at each stage of the Mass to symbolise parts of Jesus' earthly life. The similarities between these three accounts, one of which comes from the Grail legends and two from historical documents, are too striking to be dismissed as coincidence. At the same time, I found it particularly significant that such special Masses were only held on Good Friday, the day on which the Grail legends laid such store, and in the chapel of the Imperial Palace. This indicates that only a privileged few were allowed to take part in it, and that the ceremony was too solemn and sacred to be seen by all and sundry. Reading the Grail legends one is struck time and time again by the emphasis that is put upon the special sacredness of the Grail ceremonies, and how they are reserved for the King and a few privileged knights.

Thomas E. Kelley in his study of the *Perlesvaus* points out that the Shroud is actually mentioned as early as May 1204 by Hélinand, Abbot of Froidmont, albeit only obliquely. The medieval French words he uses are:

> 'Li estoires du saintisme vessel que on apele Graal o quel li precieus sans du Sauveeur fu receuz au jor qu'il fu crucifiez por le peuple racheter d'enfer . . .' (The stories of the most holy vessel called the Grail into which the precious blood of the Saviour was received on the day he was crucified to save mankind from Hell . . .).

Up to now this passage has always been taken to refer to the cup which Joseph of Arimathea is said to have drawn off the blood of Christ and which he brought to Glastonbury. In the Latin version of this passage Hélinand uses the word 'gradalis', which I have shown the lexicographers say is derived from the Latin 'cratus'. On the other hand, Medieval Latin dictionaries translate 'gradalis' as a shallow dish. Hélinand also describes the Grail in a later passage as a 'scutella lata', which is likewise translated as saucer, dish or flat bowl. In the *Quest of the Holy Grail*, the sacred vessel is likened to a shield, the Latin for which is 'scutum'. Roman shields were rectangular and slightly curved in shape. They were usually made of toughened leather stretched over a wickerwork frame. The Latin word for wickerwork is the same as that for lattice, namely 'cratis' and the words 'scutum' and its diminutive form 'scutella' come from the Sanskrit source 'skauti' meaning to cover. There is no doubt in my mind that the object to which Abbot Hélinand was referring was the shallow, platter-like casket in which the Shroud of Christ was kept, and that this was indeed the vessel into which the precious blood of the Saviour was received on the day of his crucifixion. Furthermore, Hélinand wrote these words in May 1204, less than a month after the Mandylion disappeared in the sack of Constantinople.

I next turned my attention to the *Quest of the Holy Grail*. In this version the Grail is represented as the vessel from which Jesus and his disciples ate the paschal lamb at the Last Supper:

> 'Today the Holy Grail will appear within your house and feed the companions of the Round Table . . .'
>
> 'The Holy Grail (covered with a cloth of white samite) entered through the great door and at once the palace was filled with fragrance as though all the spices of the earth had been spilled abroad. It circled the Hall along the great tables and each place was furnished in its wake with the food the occupants desired. When all were served the Holy Grail vanished they knew not where nor whither, and those that had been mute regained their speech, and many gave thanks to Our Lord for the honour he had done them in filling them with the grace of the holy vessel. But greater than all was King Arthur's joy that Our Lord should have granted him a favour given to no king before him.'

As I have just pointed out, Hélinand was not the only one to describe the Grail as a dish. Once the Shroud was removed from its shallow casket, it is easy to see how the latter could have been used as a ciborium for the celebration of a special Mass in the Real Presence of Christ. Used in this way each communicant received the Host from the very vessel in which the miraculous image of Christ's body normally rested. Such a Mass would, of course, be only celebrated on special occasions and in the presence of a privileged few. This passage is interesting for another reason. The reference to the fragrance of spices recalls what Nicolas Mesarites, Keeper of the relics in the Pharos Treasury at Constantinople had to say in 1201. In his account of the burial sindon or Shroud of Christ he tells us that it was made of linen and still smelt of myrrh. Modern forensic tests on the Shroud of Turin have likewise found traces of herbs known to have been used in Jewish burials of the first century. Finally, it is obvious that the food received by the assembled knights of the Round Table was of a spiritual nature, which filled them with the Grace of God, and that this passage has nothing to do with the common sustenance of mankind.

I have already briefly referred to the passage in this work which likens the Grail to a shield. Here it is in more detail. Forty-two years after the Passion, Joseph of Arimathea left Jerusalem and came to Sarras, a city belonging to King Evalach, who was then an infidel. Evalach was at war with his neighbour, Tholomer, but is defended by a shield 'and behold in the centre a bleeding figure of a man crucified.' Evalach overcomes Tholomer and when he returns to his city he proclaims to all people the truth that Josephus (Joseph of Arimathea's son) had shown him and bears such witness to Christ crucified that he and his family are baptised. Thenceforth Evalach takes the name of Mordrain.

Although the details differ, this story bears a remarkable resemblance to the legend of Abgar of Edessa. The shield or Grail has the power to preserve the physical body from decay and its owner from his enemies. But the similarities to the Abgar legend in this version of the Grail romance do not end here.

Lancelot comes to a ruined chapel, in which he sees a richly decked altar. He is unable to enter, so lies down outside and falls asleep. His slumber is fitful and he sees coming towards him in a litter slung between two palfreys a sick knight who is moaning aloud in anguish. As though in a trance Lancelot sees the holy vessel appear to which the sick man prays earnestly to be healed of his infirmities, so that he, too, may undertake the Quest 'wherein all good men are entered.' The Grail appears on a silver table and as soon as the sick knight sees it he falls to the ground (from where he lay in the litter) and cries out: "Gracious God, who through his Holy Vessel that I now set eyes on has performed so many miracles in this and other lands, Father, look upon me in Thy mercy and grant that I may presently be healed of my afflictions . . ." He pulls himself up until he can kiss the silver table and press his eyes to it, and at once he knows relief from his suffering. He groans aloud and says: "Ah God, I am healed."

The next story in this version of the legend speaks of Percival's encounter with his aunt, a holy recluse, who tells him how Joseph of Arimathea, his son and a company of followers come to Britain. They were short of food and met an old woman bringing twelve loaves from the bakery. When

these are portioned out among the people there is not enough
to go round and they become angry. Joseph orders the loaves
to be brought to him and tells all the people to be seated

> 'as it were at the Last Supper. And he brake the bread and
> placed pieces here and there, and at the head of the table he put
> the Holy Grail, and as he set it in place the twelve loaves were
> multiplied in such a miraculous manner that those present, who
> numbered four thousand, had every man his fill.'

It seemed absurd to me that anyone reading this passage
could pretend that the Holy Grail was the Horn of Plenty, but
so it is. Obviously the imagery doesn't fit a chalice, but who
could doubt that this is a reflection of Jesus' miracles of the
loaves and fishes as described in Matthew 13, Mark 6 and 8,
Luke 9 and John 5? Wherever you look in the *Quest* the
identification of the Grail with the body and presence of
Christ is paramount. There are numerous hidden references
to his miracles, not simply to the events of the Passion, as
though he were there in the flesh when they take place. The
vessel, in other words, is far more than the chalice of the Last
Supper; it clearly represents more than a single incident in his
life. The function of the Grail in this passage is to indicate the
Real Presence of Jesus. The Shroud in its latticework casket,
of course, is the most vivid witness to this. What the author
intends is to show that the miracles which Jesus performed on
earth can still be performed in the presence of the mysterious
image of his suffering body implanted on the Shroud.

My study of the Great Vulgate Cycle led me to consider its
authorship. This is something that has caused a lot of controversy in spite of the fact that there are quite specific statements in both the *Quest* and the *Death of King Arthur* on the
subject. Let me quote them. The last paragraph of the *Quest*
reads as follows in Dr Pauline Matarasso's translation:

> 'When they had dined King Arthur summoned his clerks who
> were keeping a record of all the adventures undergone by the
> knights of his household. When Bors had related to them the
> adventure of the Holy Grail as witnessed by himself, they were
> written down and the record kept in the library at Salisbury,
> whence Master Walter Map extracted them in order to make his

book of the Holy Grail for love of his Lord King Henry, who had the story translated from Latin into French. And with that the tale falls silent and has no more to say about the Adventures of the Holy Grail'

The first and last paragraphs of the *Death of King Arthur* in James Cable's translation reads:

'After Master Walter Map had put down in writing as much as he thought sufficient about the Adventures of the Holy Grail, his Lord King Henry II felt that what he had done would not be satisfactory unless he told about the rest of the lives of those he had previously mentioned, and the deaths of those whose prowess he had related in his book. So he began this last part; and when he put it together he called it the *Death of King Arthur* because the end of it relates how King Arthur was wounded at the battle of Salisbury and left Girflet who had long been his companion, and how no one ever again saw him alive. So Master Walter begins this last part accordingly.'

'At this point Master Walter Map will end the story of Lancelot, because he has brought everything to a proper conclusion according to the way it happened; and he finishes his book here so completely that no one can afterwards add anything to the story that is not complete falsehood.'

It struck me, when I first read these three passages, and it strikes me still, that it would be hard to find anything more unequivocal. Yet both translators and several other commentators refuse to take these statements at face value because Walter Map is known to have died in 1209 and modern scholarship is unanimous that the Great Vulgate Cycle was written between 1215 and 1235. One translator backs his opinion with the observation that the author shows only a sketchy knowledge of England; that he believes Salisbury Plain to be near the sea, and that an Englishman must have known that the monks of Glastonbury had recently (in 1191 to be precise) discovered what they claimed to be the tomb of King Arthur in the chancel of their abbey, and that he would hardly have placed Arthur's tomb in the Black Chapel by the sea. At the same time he admits that no one knows why the "true author" dissembled himself behind the identity of Map of all people, and that there are no means of dating the *Death of King Arthur* exactly. He concludes by saying that the piecing together of various scraps of information has led scholars to suppose that the work as a whole was probably written around 1230 to 1235 in France, possibly Champagne.

The other translator makes the point that the author was not a layman, but beyond that confines herself to general speculation. The text from which these translations have been made rests in the British Museum, and there is nothing to indicate whether the MSS were written by Walter Map himself or a clerk at his dictation, or later copied from earlier versions. Notwithstanding, the opinion of scholars is *not* unanimous, for the author of the article on Walter Map in the Dictionary of National Biography states, although with some reservations: "Probably the author of *Lancelot* and the *Quest of the Holy Grail*, written in French."

It was clear that I had to examine the life of Walter Map, for I was reluctant to accept the views of Dr Matarasso and Mr Cable without question. It appears that Walter Map was a native of Herefordshire or eastern Wales. There were a succession of Walter Maps at the village of Wormsley eight miles north of Hereford between 1150 and 1240, and it is likely that Master Walter was one of them. He is known for certain to have owned some land at Ullingswick close by. He was born about 1140 and went as a student to Paris in 1154 where he stayed until 1160. He returned to England before 1162 and became one of the clerks in the Royal Household. In 1179 King Henry II sent him to the Lateran Council at Rome and on the way he was hospitably entertained by Henri I, Count of Champagne, who reigned from 1152 to 1181, and who was a prominent Crusader and patron of Chrétien de Troyes. At the Council the Pope deputed him to argue with representatives of the Waldensians, a sect of heretics from Northern Italy and Switzerland, whose heresy somewhat resembled that of the Cathars.

At one time or another during his career, Walter Map was a canon of St Paul's Cathedral in London, of Lincoln Cathedral and of Hereford, Precentor of Lincoln and later Chancellor of that diocese. In 1197 he was appointed Archdeacon of Oxford. He was at Chinon in France on July 6 1189 when King Henry

II died, with which his connection with the Court seems to have ended.

Consequently, if the three statements I have just quoted are to be believed, Master Walter must have set down his account of the legends between 1162 and 1189, during the lifetime of his Lord, King Henry II.

Englishmen tend to forget that Henry II and his son Richard Coeur de Lion spent much the greater part of their lives outside England. They saw themselves as first and foremost French princes who happened to own a valuable "colony" in Britain. They ruled their vast domains, about which I shall have a great deal to say later, not so much from London as from Rouen. Consequently a man like Master Walter, who first came to France at the age of 14 and remained outside England with his King almost continuously for the next thirty-five years, can be pardoned for thinking that Salisbury Plain is near the sea. From the point of view of someone living in Eastern France or on the Loire, it is. So, for that matter, is Glastonbury. This criticism of Master Walter seems to stem from a certain insularity on the part of those who question his knowledge of English geography. Master Walter's benefices in Lincoln, London and Herefore need not have claimed much of his personal attention. Many valuable ecclesiastical positions were held *in absentia*. So until 1189 there is every reason to believe that he seldom came to Britain.

But the matter doesn't rest there. Walter Map is best remembered for his *"De Nugis Curialium"*, a sort of Latin gossip column made up of tales of his native country and anecdotes of Court life. He wrote it between 1182 and 1192, and he has a lot to say about the Templars among other things. In brief, Walter was an efficient, sophisticated civil servant, who was trusted by his King; who travelled widely in Europe, and who was at home in the intellectual and cultural milieux of his time.

If you have read thus far you will have noticed that I have been concentrating on those descriptions of the Grail which appear to refer to the Shroud/Mandylion in its golden, lattice-work casket. But what, you may ask, about Wolfram's description of it as a magic stone? Wolfram says that he derived his account of the story of Parsifal and the Grail from one Kyot, whom he described as "ein Provenzal". I quickly discovered that oceans of ink have been spilled in the attempt to identify Kyot. The term "Provenzal" seems at first sight to indicate someone from Provence, but no troubadour or minstrel of that name is known to historians. Otto Rahn, on the other hand, had no doubt about it: Kyot was none other than Guiot de Provins, a thirteenth century troubadour from Champagne, whose best known work is a satyrical poem he called *La Bible*. As I said in chapter one, much of Rahn's work is highly suspect, but in this instance I have to admit that his case is a good one.

I had forgotten that Wolfram admits somewhere in his poem *Parzival* that he was largely ignorant of languages other than his native German, and that he could barely read and write. There was nothing out of the ordinary in this, for many troubadours and minnesingers committed their ballads to memory, and it was only later that they were written down. Nevertheless this was an important factor I had to bear in mind when I came to consider the words and names Wolfram uses.

The first thing I noticed was that Wolfram is very vague when he comes to describe the Grail. He makes it plain that it was a means of concealing something of great consequence, which is a description that would admirably fit the latticework casket enclosing the Shroud. He also seems to be describing a specially sacred Mass when he writes:

> 'A hundred squires took break in white napkins from before the Grail . . . and passed it to all the tables.'

On the other hand he makes Parsifal's uncle, Trevrizent, describe the Grail as a kind of stone, which Wolfram calls by its Latin name. This has caused people a lot of trouble, because the surviving texts of the poem differ at this point. The St Gall manuscript calls it 'Lapsit exillis' where all the others have variants. 'Lapsit' varies with 'lapis' and 'iaspis' which mean stone and jasper, and 'exillis' varies with 'exilis', 'ereillis', 'erilis', 'exilix' and 'exillix'. Only 'exilis' and 'erilis' are proper Latin words, the former meaning thin, lean or slender, the latter meaning literally heir, or more properly 'of the master' or 'of the mistress'.

You will remember that in the legend of Abgar of Edessa the miraculous towel transferred its portrait of Jesus to a tile outside Hierapolis and to another during the relic's long sojourn over the city gate of Edessa. You will also remember that both the cloth and the tile, then called the Mandylion and Keramion respectively, were brought to Constantinople in the year 944 and housed in the Pharos and Blachernae chapels.

No picture of the Keramion is known to exist, but from what we know of it, it is not hard to guess its size. It must have been large enough to cover the cloth in Abgar's golden, lattice-work casket, for the story tells us that the bishop of Edessa put it on top to keep out the damp before he sealed up the niche. Consequently, as we know the size of the Shroud, and hence of the folded Mandylion, it is not unreasonable to think that the Keramion measured about four feet by two, unless it was placed over the face area alone, in which case it would have been about two feet square. In either case it must have been thin, since all tiles are. Could the Keramion have been Wolfram's 'Lapis exilis' or thin stone? It certainly seems possible. There are, however, two other stones associated with the burial of Jesus. One was the Stone of Unction, upon which his body was laid for annointing before burial, and the other was the great stone which was rolled in front of the tomb. The former was depicted on the eucharistic embroidered cloths used in the Byzantine rite. These cloths show Jesus laid out in death in the manner of the Shroud. The latter came to be sym-bolised by the cover of the chalice used at the celebration of Mass. It is hard to say which of these three stones Wolfram had in mind, but he specifically associates his stone Grail with Good Friday:

'Always on Good Friday (the dove) brings a white wafer to the Stone . . .'

It seems that Wolfram had two objects in mind to which he

applied the term 'Graal'. His knowledge of French was
sketchy, so if he had read Chrétien's poem, or, what is more
likely, had someone read it to him, it is hardly surprising that
he failed to grasp the true meaning of the word he wrote as
'Graal'. I have been puzzled by the extent to which this mis-
understanding on Wolfram's part might have gone. If
Chrétien and Wolfram knew of the existence of the Mandylion
casket and the Keramion but had not actually seen them, they
would almost certainly have known their close historical
association, for Ordericus Vitalis had told the story of Abgar
in his great history of the Church. As this was widely read
throughout western Europe, any moderately educated man
such as Wolfram and Chrétien would surely have heard it.
Wolfram might not have known that the Keramion and the
Mandylion were housed in separate places in Constantinople,
so he would have given the one term 'Graal' to them both,
believing them to be kept together in the latticework casket.
Furthermore, Wolfram reproaches Chrétien for inaccuracy,
and we are forced to ask whether the absence of any mention
of a stone Grail in the latter's work might be one of the things
Wolfram complains of. We must not forget that the Grail was
not the Shroud itself or the Keramion, but the 'cratis' or
'greil'; that is to say, the latticework casket in which the
former was kept. This is something which has been forgotten
since the disappearance of the Mandylion in 1204.

R.S. Loomis thinks that Wolfram assumed the Stone and
the Grail were one and the same, and though this leads him to
trace the origin of the latter to a legend relating to Alexander
the Great, this can now be discounted, since Loomis knew
nothing of the Shroud's history, and certainly never thought of
the Grail in terms of a latticework casket.

On the other hand, did Wolfram intentionally or acci-
dentally misunderstand the true nature of the Grail? He tells
us that in its presence each man obtained whatever he held his
hand out for. The *Quest* asserts that as the vessel passed before
the tables, the knights were instantly filled with such food as
they desired. In another version the vessel brought to the holy
in life all the good viands the heart of man could desire. I find
it hard to understand why so many commentators should take
all this so literally. After all, when Christians speak of eating

Christ's flesh and drinking his blood no one nowadays
seriously thinks of them as cannibals! Why, then, should they
take passages such as these? Maybe they seem a bit
exaggerated to us today, but we do not know enough of the
medieval mind to tell how they appeared to contemporaries of
Chrétien and Wolfram. In the light of my definition, however,
the Grail as a dish or tray makes a good deal more sense than
would a cup or chalice.

The first sequel to the *Conte del Graal*, probably written
between 1180 and 1200 illustrates this very well. Gawain
enters a great hall and sees a bier on which lay a corpse with
half a sword-blade on it. A priest enters bearing a cross and
over his alb he wears a tunic of 'precious cloth of Constantinople'. He and his acolytes conduct a Mass for the Dead.
The priest leaves and the king, accompanied by a large crowd
(the same as those who attended the Requiem) enters and
they sit down to eat. They are served by the Grail. This 'feast'
suggests that here we have an example of the latticework
casket being used as a salver from which each communicant
receives the Host as though directly from Jesus himself. The
Requiem and the 'Feast' are to some extent symbolic, for the
company suddenly vanishes leaving Gawain by himself with
the bier and the bleeding Lance, which is subsequently
identified as that which pierced Jesus' side on the Cross. The
Grail is differentiated from the bier, which shows that the
Shroud may have been laid out on a bier-like structure while
the casket in which it normally reposed was used as a
Ciborium for the Mass.

A.E. Waite has made an exhaustive study of the Grail
legends and their symbolism. He points out that the legend
depends upon certain values attaching to various sacred
objects. The most important of these is the Grail itself. The
others include the Lance and the Sword. The fourth is the dish
which he finds the most difficult to define, since he assumes
that the Grail was the cup of the Last Supper. Of all these
sacred objects, the Sword and the Lance present the least
difficulty, as these are recorded among the relics in the Pharos
Treasury. I have discussed the identity of the dish at some
length, and hope to have shown that this, too, was among the
same collection of relics. What of the cup?

There are several versions of the Cup legend. Following the Ascension of Christ his earthly body was removed from the world; there remained the holy vessel into which his blood had been received by Joseph of Arimathea. Endowed with the virtues of the risen Christ and the power of the Holy Ghost, it sustained him spiritually for forty years of imprisonment. After his release the holy vessel became the sign of saving grace to a certain number of initiates Joseph had elected to take westward with him to Britain. There the other sacred objects were added to it and all of them were held in a secret place.

The term "vessel" is, of course, neutral and can just as well apply to a cup as to a latticework casket. But assuming for the moment that it refers to the cup, according to the Gospel of Nicodemus, one of the apocryphal accounts of Jesus' ministry not included in the New Testament, but nevertheless a very early work, Joseph of Arimathea had made the vessel before Good Friday and had come with it ready for the crucifixion. According to this account Joseph collected the blood while Jesus was on the Cross, and while the blood was still flowing from his wounds. As blood stops flowing after the heart stops beating, the only way to collect it was while Jesus was still alive, and the only vessel it could be collected in would have been a cup. Yet we know that the body was taken down from the cross and buried in a hurry because of the imminence of the Passover, so it is not unreasonable to suppose that traces of the blood would pass on to the burial cloths. This is precisely what we can now see on the Shroud of Turin. Consequently there are traces of blood in the latticework Grail, so the distinction between cup and casket is now blurred.

Those who followed Chrétien wavered in their understanding between the notion of a paschal dish and a cup in which Christ consecrated the wine of the first Eucharist. If our medieval ancestors believed in the authenticity of the Mandylion, the Lance, the Sword and the Crown of Thorns, (and there is no doubt at all that they did) then the existence of a Cup of the Last Supper is no less likely. Robert de Boron says the vessel is

'a reliquary which shall henceforth be called a Chalice' :

'Cist vaisseau ou men sanc meis
Quant de men cors le requiellis
Calices apelez sera.'

Waite's commentary makes fascinating reading in the light of
my hypothesis. This is what he says:

'It is difficult to read the later verses in which the Eucharistic
Chalice is compared with the Sepulchre of Christ, the Mass
Corporal with the grave-clothes, and the Paten with the stone at
the mouth of the tomb, without concluding that by the Grail
there was intended the first Eucharistic vessel . . . If it be
objected that this idea of a Chalice does not correspond to a
vessel, the content of which is sacramental wine, it should be
rememberred that a reliquary which by the hypothesis contained the precious Blood was obviously in sacramental
correspondence with Eucharistic wine . . . It seems certain that
when Robert de Boron speaks of the Grail as a vessel *in* which
Christ made his sacrament, this ought to be understood as referring to the Paschal Dish.'

Substititute in your mind's eye, the casket with the Shroud
within it; remember what modern research has told us about
the image on the Shroud, and the medical evidence which
explains the marks of blood and lacerations on the body, and
read the above passage again. This vessel must be the latticework casket; it does contain the grave-clothes in which Jesus
made his supreme sacrifice. There is no further need for
intellectual contortions.

But let us look at this a little closer. The *Lesser Holy Grail*
speaks of

'The great secret uttered at the great sacrament performed *over*
the Grail – that is over the Chalice.'

But that makes nonsense. The sacrament is not celebrated
over a chalice but with one. It can, however, be celebrated at
an altar containing a relic such as the Shroud. The *Greater Holy
Grail*, even when it reproduces de Boron, gives an explanation
of the sacred vessel as a dish in which Jesus partook of the Last
Supper. At first sight this seems preposterous, since no dish
could at the same time be a reliquary which is essentially a

hollow object for keeping relics in. On the other hand, the Byzantine reproductions of the Mandylion which I discussed in chapter two do make it appear as if Jesus' head were resting on a dish, and even the casket itself must have been somewhat dish-like in shape, since it is unlikely to have been more than a few inches deep. The blessed reliquary of the *Greater Holy Grail* would seem to have been rather the outward witness of what was within it. The first unveiled vision of it is a chapel with an altar on one side of which were the Nails used at the Crucifixion together with the Holy Lance; on the other side was a dish and in the centre there was an 'exceeding rich vessel of gold in the semblance of a goblet.' But can we be quite certain that the word translated here as 'goblet' was originally written as 'cratus' or 'cratis'? Anyone ignorant of the true nature of the casket in which the Shroud was kept would naturally think that the word written as 'cratis' or 'gradella' were mistakes for the more familiar 'cratus' or 'gradalus'.

While I was reading Robert de Clari's account of Constantinople, I was struck by the following passage which must surely be the origin of some of these descriptions of the Grail chapel which we find in the romances. De Clari wrote this in 1205, after he had spent nearly two years in Constantinople during which time he witnessed the pillaging of the city by the barbarous Frankish soldiery. He is writing of the Pharos Treasury where the Mandylion was usually kept.

> 'The Holy Chapel . . . was so rich and noble that there was not a hinge nor a band nor any other part such as is usually made of iron that was not all of silver, and there was no column that was not of jasper or porphyry or some other rich precious stone. And the pavement of this chapel was so rich and so noble that no one could ever tell you its great beauty and nobility. Within this chapel were found many rich relics. There were two pieces of the True Cross as large as the leg of a man and as long as half a *toise*; there was also the iron of the Lance with which Our Lord had his side pierced and two of the nails which were driven through his hands and feet. There was in a crystal phial quite a little of his blood; there was a tunic which he wore and which was taken from him when they led him to the Mount of Calvary; there was the blessed Crown with which he was

crowned which was made of reeds with thorns as sharp as the
points of daggers ... Now there is still another relic in this
chapel which we had forgotten to tell you about. For there were
two rich vessels of gold hanging in the midst of the chapel by two
heavy silver chains. In one of these vessels there was a tile and in
the other a cloth ...'

The *Greater Holy Grail* goblet is said to have had a lid 'after the
manner of a ciborium'. A ciborium is a receptacle for the
reservation of the Host. It is usually in the shape of a box,
though it can be cup-shaped. If this is indeed a reflection of de
Clari's description of the Pharos Treasury, then the goblet
could be, perhaps, the phial of holy blood. However, the word
de Clari uses is 'fiole', translated here as 'phial', and these
words derive from the Greek φιάλη which originally meant a
flat vessel or dish.

In the *Roman du Saint Graal* the blood was 'drawn into the
vessel after Joseph and Nicodemus had taken down the body
of the Lord.' Medically speaking this makes nonsense, since,
as I have already said, blood ceases to flow when the heart
stops beating, so if this statement is to be taken at face value,
two things follow: either Jesus was not dead when he was
taken down from the Cross, or the blood was not drawn into
the vessel. On the other hand, if the vessel were the Shroud,
then the blood got on to it after the body had been wrapped in
it, but since the shroud was not put into a vessel of any kind
until long afterwards, this statement cannot be literally true.

Before I leave this subject there is one more passage I want
to consider. It comes from the *Perlesvaus*, which I touched upon
briefly in chapter one. It concerns the radiance that Sir
Gawain seemed to see within the Grail. Modern scientific
research has been unable to explain how the image of Christ
comes to be on the Shroud. The nearest anyone has come so
far is to say that it resembles a scorch, and must have been
made by heat or light. I am not prepared to go along with
those who see in this a proof of the resurrection. All I am
prepared to say is that so far, science has not been able to
come up with a naturalistic explanation. Nevertheless, in the
course of this investigation I have been struck by the
recurrence of references to fire and radiance in connection

with the Shroud. There was the incident of the fire at Hierapolis when Ananias hid under a heap of tiles the cloth that Jesus had given him to take to Abgar; there was the miraculous transference of the image of the face from the Mandylion to the Keramion while it was walled up in Edessa; there are countless references in the legends to light and radiance in connection with the Grail.

It is a well-attested fact that those who possess the power of healing are unanimous in saying that they are conscious, as Jesus said himself, of the 'goodness' going out of them when they effect any cure. I have seen with my own eyes the red marks left by the hands of an old Dordogne peasant who brings relief to arthritic patients simply by laying his hands on the afflicted part. In that highly irreverent book *"The Keys of St Peter"* by Roger Peyrefitte there is a passage which seems to me to be relevant in this connection. The incident I am about to quote follows a flippant conversation about the marks made by souls in Purgatory. The young, starry-eyed seminarist, Victor Mas, is taken to see some of them:

> 'They crossed the nave. In a room next the sacristy, the doors of a cupboard were opened for them; this revealed illuminated showcases containing bits of wood, books and pieces of cloth upon which appeared the terrible imprints in question. Some looked like cigarette burns, others as if they had been made by hot curling irons. There was the end of a skirt that had belonged to a Westphalian nun and received its burns from the soul of another nun in 1696. There was also the tail of a chemise that had belonged to the abbess of Todi, and upon which an abbot of Mantua had left the imprint of his burning hands in 1731. There, too, was the shirt of a Belgian whose deceased mother had left a similar mark on it in June 1789 . . .'

All this, and more, is written very much with tongue in cheek, nevertheless the point I want to make is this: the idea of radiance attached to relics is a very common one, and there are very many references to this in medieval and later literature.

In the course of the same episode from the *Perlesvaus* a change is made in the aspect of the external object, which appeared "all in flesh'. This must mean that it was transformed before Sir Gawain's eyes into a vision of Christ crucified. This closely corresponds to an unfolding of the Mandylion cloth into the full-length Shroud as described by Robert de Clari.

Before I leave this commentary on the Grail legends there is one final point to notice; it is the role played by women in the Grail ceremonials. I have already quoted several instances where two maidens enter with the Grail, which is described as a dish or salver on which is a man's head surrounded by blood. Chrétien refers somewhere to the Grail as a deepish platter borne by two maidens, large enough to hold a lamprey or salmon, but with merely a single wafer in it. These fish grow to a length of between three or four feet, and I have calculated the dimensions of the latticework casket as four feet by two feet. Some commentators have found this association of women with the celebration of the Eucharist almost inexplicable. I find it nothing of the sort. When one remembers that the Grail casket contained the Shroud of Christ, and when one recalls that it was Mary Magdalene, Mary the mother of James, Joanna and Salome who went to the tomb and found it empty, it would be almost more curious if such a Mass were celebrated without the presence of women. There is another point, too. The image of Christ within the Grail casket could be taken to symbolize the infant Jesus within the womb of Mary, and it is highly significant that the Mandylion and so many reproductions of it should be found in churches dedicated to the Mother of God.

It is now time to turn our attention to the history of France in the twelfth and thirteenth centuries to see what this can tell us about the Grail legends.

# PART TWO
*Why King Arthur?*

# FOUR

THE THIRD DECADE of the twlefth century saw the appearance of two important books; one was Geoffrey of Monmouth's History of the Kings of Britain which contained an account of the reign of King Arthur, the other was the monumental history of the Church by Ordericus Vitalis which mentioned the Mandylion/Shroud. Is this purely coincidental or was there some connection? I must confess that I can come to no definite conclusion, but it did seem necessary to try to find out why the Arthurian story should become so popular at this particular time, and why the legend of the Grail was grafted on to it.

The politics of France and England at this time were dominated for more than thirty years by the rivalry between King Stephen and Queen Matilda for the English throne and for a further fifty by the rise and fall of the Angevin Empire. Throughout the period Europe was engaged in the Crusades against the Moslem princes in Palestine, which arose from the deep consciousness of the threat that Islam posed to Christianity. In some respects this period resembled our own, for the fundamental struggle was one of East versus West. Consequently people were acutely aware not only of their historical heroes but also of the importance of their religion.

When Prince William, the son and heir of King Henry I of England was drowned in the *White ship* in 1120, there arose the spectre of a disputed succession in both England and Normandy. There were two claimants: the King's daughter,

49

Matilda, widow of the Holy Roman Emperor Henry V and wife of Geoffrey Plantagenet, Count of Anjou, and Stephen, the son of William the Conqueror's daughter, Adela by Stephen Henry of Blois, Count of Champagne. This rivalry for the English throne meant that even though Matilda's husband eventually became Duke of Normandy, there was no serious Anglo-Norman pressure on the French King, Louis VII, until after King Stephen's death in 1154. At that period Champagne was a principality nominally under the suzerainty of the King of France, but in reality independent. Theobald IV, Count of Champagne took the side of Pope Innocent II in his quarrel with the French king over the latter's right to nominate a new Archbishop of Bourges. He also sided with his brothers, King Stephen of England and Henry of Blois, who was Abbot of Glastonbury and Bishop of Winchester, in their disputes with King Louis, who was their suzerain in France.

Louis VII has been dismissed as a weak king, but in fact he was both courageous and a realist, if somewhat bookish. The only way he could make peace with the Pope was to undertake some kind of penance, and the obvious one was to go on a Crusade. In 1146, St Bernard, who was then preaching throughot France to great effect, persuaded Louis to set out with his Queen, Eleanor of Aquitaine, on what turned out to be the disastrous Second Crusade, which lasted from 1147 to 1149. They were accompanied by a great throng of knights, noblemen and princes, and arrived in Constantinople in October 1147, where the French King and Queen were received with great courtesy by the Byzantine Emperor. Among their retinue were Everard de Barre, the Grand Master of the Order of Knights Templar and Henry, the eldest son and heir of Theobald, Count of Champagne. King Louis and Queen Eleanor were lodged in the Philopatium palace and entertained to banquets at the Blachernae. They were also conducted round the city by the Emperor. In the course of this visit the relics of the Passion housed in the Boukoleon and Blachernae palaces were shown to the French King and leading members of his entourage, including the Grand Master and Henry of Champagne.

The following spring King Louis and Queen Eleanor set out

once more and reached Antioch in April 1148. Here her indiscreet behaviour with Raymond of Tripoli, her uncle, caused a great scandal. Alarmed for his honour, Louis dragged his wife from her uncle's bed and carried her off to Jerusalem. These and other quarrels wrought havoc among the Crusaders to the point where the great expedition suffered a crushing defeat at the hands of the Moslems and was forced to retire. Early the next year, realising that his wife's behaviour would compel him to divorce her, Louis decided to return to France. They left in the early summer by sea and landed in southern Italy at the end of July. On the way, the King's fleet was attacked by a Byzantine squadron, and a ship containing many of his followers was taken as a war-prize to Constantinople. This action had far-reaching consequences.

Throughout his overland journey to France, Louis fulminated against what he regarded as a wanton act of perfidy on the part of the Byzantines, urging the Pope and anyone else who would listen, to launch a new crusade against the Emperor Manuel. The catastrophic failure of the Second Crusade, henceforth, was blamed on Byzantine treachery, and it became an article of faith to take vengeance on these traitors to Christendom. Here, then, was one origin of the quarrel which culminated fifty-five years later in the sack of Constantinople by the French and Venetians. There were other reasons too. The sight of the riches of Constantinople had excited the greed of the Frenchmen, and it was not only the gold and jewels they had seen, but also the astonishing collection of relics stored away in the Pharos and Blachernae Treasuries.

In an age when tourism took the form of pilgrimages to shrines such as Compostella, Rome or the Holy Land, the holiness of relics meant big business. The holier the object the bigger the income, so relics of the Passion were by far the greatest in potential value. The discovery of the extent of the relic collection in Constantinople set off the same greedy stampede as the gold of Mexico and Peru did four hundred years later. The race was now on to see who could capture these glittering prizes first. The quest for the Holy Grail, in other words, took on the aspect of a gold rush.

In 1152 Louis VII finally divorced Eleanor of Aquitaine, not on the grounds of adultery with her uncle, but on the specious grounds of consanguinity (they were very distant cousins). She had borne the king two daughters, Marie and Alix, who were destined to be the wives of the two sons of Theobald IV of Champagne; Henry, who succeeded his father as Count of Champagne, and Theobald who was created Count of Blois and Chartres. Less than two months after her divorce, Eleanor pulled off the coup of the age by marrying the nineteen-year-old Henry Plantagenet, the son of Matilda and Geoffrey. To his considerable lands, which included the Counties of Anjou, Touraine and Maine and the Duchy of Normandy, she brought the whole of south-western France as far as the Pyrenees. Their joint domains came to be known as the Angevin Empire, which stretched from the Cheviots to the

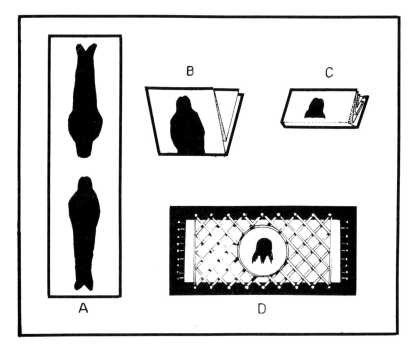

Shroud folded into Mandylion

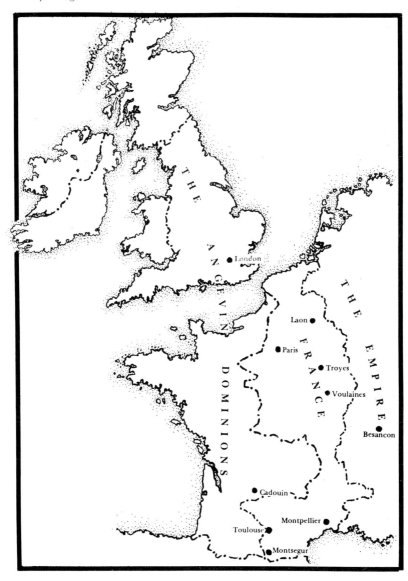

The Angevin Empire

borders of Spain. Eleanor was thirty, of outstanding beauty, and of a domineering character. The marriage was without doubt the triumph of the younger generation and an inspiration to every up-and-coming nobleman in France.

It is hardly surprising that Louis VII felt aggrieved. Not only had Eleanor failed to bear him a son; at a stroke she had lost him more than half his kingdom. King Stephen of England disputed Henry Plantagent's title to Normandy, and Stephen's brother, Theobald of Champagne also rallied to the side of King Louis. A month after the marriage all these enemies converged on Normandy, but the youthful Henry beat them back. In January 1153 he was strong enough to cross over into England, where he was eagerly welcomed by a populace grown weary of the long civil war between Stephen and Matilda. Compelling the ailing Stephen to name him his heir, Henry II ascended the English throne the following year.

In the course of the next half dozen years, Eleanor bore Henry II three sons who survived to play important roles in the history of France. Henry, the eldest, surnamed Courtmantel, but also known as the "Young King", was born in 1155. Richard, afterwards known as Coeur de Lion, was born in 1157, and Geoffrey, later Duke of Brittany, in 1158. Nine years later she bore him a fourth son, John, surnamed Lackland, his father's favourite son and England's most ignoble king.

The first twenty-five years of Henry II's reign, which included the murder of Thomas à Becket, do not concern us here, except that eight years after he came to the throne of England, Walter Map joined his Household. Consequently, Master Walter would have been a close observer of all that went on during this time. During the 1170s he would have witnessed the rebellion of the King's sons; the acknowledgement of Richard as heir to his mother's dukedom of Aquitaine; the coronation in the old King's lifetime, of the "Young King", Henry Courtmantel; the marriage of the "Young King" to the Princess Marguerite, daughter of Louis VII by his second wife; the death of the "Young King" and the remarriage of his widow to King Bela III of Hungary; and the adoption by King Henry II of his third son, Geoffrey as his heir in preference to his second son, Richard. All these events have a bearing on the story of the Grail as I was soon to discover. At the age of eight, Geoffrey was betrothed to Constance, the daughter of Duke Conan of Brittany, and in 1175, when he was eighteen, he did homage to his father on a promise of half the revenues of the dukedom. From now onward he was known as the Duke of Brittany and acknowledged heir to the Angevin Empire.

After his divorce from Eleanor, King Louis VII married Constance of Castile by whom he had two more daughters, one of whom, Marguerite, I have already mentioned. On the death of Constance he married Adela of Champagne, by whom he at last had a son, Philippe, who succeeded him as King of France in 1180.

When Philippe ascended the throne his first task was to gain control of his over-powerful feudatories, the Dukes of Normandy, Burgundy and Guyenne and the Counts of Champagne, Flanders and Toulouse. His next priority was to break up the Angevin Empire. In this he cleverly exploited the Freudian situation which existed in the family of King Henry II of England, where Eleanor dominated her four sons to the point of inciting them to rebellion against their father. Philippe even went to the length of sharing his bed with Richard, of whom, in his youth, he seems genuinely to have been fond. In the end, of course, the four Plantagenet princes succeeded in ruining their own fortunes, as so often happens to the sons of rich and successful parents. They kept great state; they had a host of hangers-on; they were tempted, even against their own true interest, to struggle for whatever they could get. They became the idols of their generation. Thanks to this, Philippe was able to surmount all his dangers, though luck played its part. Henry, the "Young King" died in 1183; Geoffrey, Duke of Brittany, three years later.

This left Richard and John, then a child of little consequence. Within six years of his accession, therefore, the political situation in France had changed dramatically in Philippe's favour. He had waged successful wars against the Count of Flanders and the Duke of Burgundy, in the course of which he captured the great stronghold of Vergy, near Dijon, and forced these over-mighty vassals into submission.

On the death of Geoffrey Plantagenet in 1186 a dispute at

once arose over the lordship of Brittany. However, Geoffrey's widow gave birth to a son, Arthur, who thus became heir not only to his father's dukedom, but also to those of his grand-father, King Henry II, should his uncle, Richard Coeur de Lion fail to produce an heir of his own. Since everyone knew of Richard's sexual proclivities, the chances of his doing so were remote. This, then, was the situation when news came early in 1187 of Saladin's successful attack on the Frankish kingdoms in the Holy Land, the capture of the Prince of Antioch and of the Grand Masters of the Templars and of the Knights of St John. The scene was set for the Third Crusade.

The political situation can be briefly summed up: Henry II of England was fifty-four and approaching old age. His eldest and third sons had died, leaving his second, homosexual and childless son, Richard, as heir. His youngest, favourite son, John was then aged nineteen. John was the unknown factor, but with the birth of Prince Arthur, an heir to the Angevin Empire had been born upon whom all hopes for the future could be pinned. Richard was still in the prime of life and could be expected to live for many years to come, but until the end of the century, waiting in the background, was Arthur, Duke of Brittany, son of the widow of Geoffrey Plantagenet. To King Philippe Arthur represented the chance to regain all that his father had lost after he divorced Eleanor; to the English and to the supporters of Richard, Arthur was the lawful heir to the mightiest European Empire since Charlemagne's.

The troubadours such as Chrétien de Troyes, were not slow to see the implications of this situation. It is no wonder that Perceval, the hero of the Arthurian legends should be called the son of the widow of Anjou. On the death of Richard Coeur de Lion in 1199, the fourteen year-old Arthur ought to have come into his inheritance. In fact the unfortunate lad became a pawn in the power struggle between his uncle, John Lackland and King Philippe. John seized the throne of England and then the person of his young nephew. Within a few weeks Arthur had been murdered. The crime was so heinous that ever since King John has come to typify the arch-wicked uncle, and at the time Prince Arthur became a martyr and the archetype of innocent youth.

Even before the birth of Prince Arthur of Brittany, King
Henry II had found it politic to foster tales of British glory to
rival the splendour which stories about Charlemagne shed on
his descendant, the French king. The links between Celtic
Brittany and Celtic Britain were strengthened, and the
heroism of Arthur was matched against the heroism of
Charlemagne. The popularity of these stories, therefore, had a
strongly political aspect; the Grail was introduced for equally
material and practical reasons. Not to put too fine a point
upon it, he who obtained the most priceless relic of all, namely
the Shroud of Christ, obtained the greatest religious, political
and economic asset of all, and there were three contenders in
the field – the Papacy, the King of France and the Order of
Knights Templar. With the capture of Jerusalem by Saladin
in the autumn of 1187 the way was open for another Crusade,
in the course of which who knew what opportunities there
might not be to avenge the Byzantine treachery of 1149 and to
capture the holiest and most valuable relics of Christendom.
In any such venture there were bound to be alliances among
the three contenders, and both the King of France and the
Papacy were ready to woo the Templars whose wealth placed
them in a commanding position to set the price of their
support. On the sidelines stood Richard of England, the hero
of the age, the ideal of chivalry and courage. The stories of
King Arthur, of Perceval and of the Knights of the Round
Table became to a large extent mirrors of the times and
propaganda in the struggle between these rivalries.

In 1190 King Philippe and King Richard set off together for
the Holy Land, but jealous rivalry soon broke out between
them. Philippe, having promised to respect Richard's French
domains returned home. In passing through Rome he
shamelessly tried to persuade the Pope to release him from his
promise to Richard. The Pope refused. By now Richard had
declared Arthur to be his heir, and out of spite John Lackland
at once allied himself with Philippe. After performing feats of
military genius, Richard faced up to realities and made his
peace with Saladin. On his way home he was captured and
made prisoner by the German Emperor. This was the signal
for Philippe and John to attack his lands in France. They did

all they could to persuade the Emperor to hold on to his royal captive. But Richard's friends rallied round and raised a ransom. In February 1194 he finally reached England, where he was re-crowned, gathered an army and once more set out to fight for the lands he had lost in France.

Richard's southern neighbour was Count Raymond V of Toulouse, whose lands comprised Languedoc and Provence, extending from the eastern Pyrenees as far east as the Rhone along the southern borders of Aquitaine. Like the Count of Champagne and the Duke of Burgundy, Raymond was a virtually independent prince although nominally a vassal of the King of France. There had been constant friction between the Counts of Toulouse and the Dukes of Aquitaine, but at this juncture of his affairs, Richard determined to ally himself to Raymond. The latter patched up his quarrels with the King of Aragon, his neighbour to the south, and united with Richard against their common overlord, the King of France. The alliance was cemented by the marriage of Richard's sister, Jeanne Plantagenet to Raymond's son, the future Raymond VI. In the course of these negotiations Richard visited Toulouse and Carcassonne, where he met the famous Adelaide de Burlat, who was then ruling that city as regent for her young son, Ramon-Roger de Trencavel. From Carcassonne Richard went to Beaucaire on the Rhone for his sister's wedding, an event to which all the nobility and troubadours of Provence, Languedoc, Aquitaine and Champagne were invited. It is said that more than ten thousand knights and troubadours attended the festivities which lasted nearly a month.

Following the "Fête de Beaucaire" Richard and Raymond declared war on the King of France, but in April 1199 a chance arrow fired from the walls of the castle of Chalus near Limoges struck Richard in the shoulder. Gangrene set in, and, faced with death, he sent for his mother. The castle was taken and the archer who had shot him was brought before the King, who chivalrously pardoned him and gave him some money. In one of his purpler passages, Sir Winston Churchill described the death of Richard in these words:

> "On April 6th 1199 he died, worthy by the consent of all men to sit with King Arthur and Roland and other heroes of martial

romance at some Eternal Round Table, which we trust the Creator of the Universe in His comprehension will not have forgotten to provide.

The archer was flayed alive."

You will recall that Wolfram von Eschenbach attributed his knowledge of the Grail legend to one Kyot, whom some commentators identify with Guiot de Provins, whose most famous work was a satyrical poem entitled *La Bible*. This poem was written in the 1190s and in it he lists his many patrons. These include Louis VII, Henry II of England, Richard Coeur de Lion, Henry Courtmantel, the "Young King" and Raymond V of Toulouse. It is not known for certain whether he attended the Fête de Beaucaire, but it is certain that he travelled extensively throughout France, Germany, Aquitaine, Languedoc and Aragon. In 1184, for instance, he was at a gathering of knights and troubadours at Mainz, where it is possible that he may have met Wolfram. He was at the Court of Henry II, so it is highly probable that he also met Walter Map. I shall return to this later. For the moment it is enough to say that these political events must have been known by at least three of the authors of the Grail romances, Chrètien de Troyes, Walter Map and Wolfram von Eschenbach if they were not actually witnessed by them. They would also have known that the House of Plantagenet at that time was held to possess supernatural ancestry. Richard's feats of arms certainly lent credence to the belief. People hoped that young Arthur of Brittany would carry on the tradition of his forefathers. Is it any wonder, then, that the romancers should have chosen the Plantagenets (or the House of Anjou as they thinly disguised them) as the one from which the hero Perceval descended?

In 1197 the German Emperor, Henry VI, died at the age of thirty-two while planning a new Crusade. The new Pope, Innocent III was only thirty-seven when he was elected. He thus found himself in the unusual position for a Pope of having no lay rival, since the election of a successor to the Emperor had not yet taken place. He was quick to consolidate his position.

Innocent III began his reign by preaching the new Crusade,

and as a preliminary step opened negotiations with the Byzantine Emperor, Alexius III, over the union of the Churches. He sent agents to France and Germany, but recruitment was more restricted than before, but many of those who were moved to take the cross, did so less out of piety than out of a wish to acquire land or riches. Theobald V of Champagne was the generally acknowledged leader; with him went Baldwin IX of Flanders, Louis, Count of Blois and many other knights and barons from northern France and Burgundy including the three brothers, Geoffrey, Simon and André de Joinville, Clérambault de Noyers and Henri de Vergy.

The expedition took a long time to organise, and in 1201 Theobald of Champagne died suddenly and was succeeded as leader of the Crusade by an Italian nobleman, Boniface, Marquis of Montferrat. The scene was set for the sack of Constantinople.

In that city, meanwhile, the Emperor Isaac Angelos had married the ten-year-old daughter of King Bela III of Hungary, Margaret, who on her marriage took the additional name of Mary in accordance to the custom of Byzantium. In 1195, ten years after the wedding, Isaac was deposed in a palace revolution by his brother, Alexius, and thrown into prison with his wife and two young sons, where his eyes were torn out. Towards the end of 1202, the elder of these sons, likewise called Alexius, escaped and fled to Germany, where he made a treaty with Boniface de Montferrat and the other leaders of the Crusade, by which they agreed to attack Byzantium and to restore him to his father's throne.

Thus, at last, the chance for which so many of the French nobles and princes had been waiting for more than fifty years had come. By backing the young Alexius they could make the Eastern Empire a client of the Western and help themselves to the treasures of the most fabulous city on earth. Now was the time to acquire by fair means or foul some of the priceless relics which the Kings and Popes of the west had longed to possess. The Quest for the Holy Grail was about to become a rape.

The Crusader army eventually arrived before the walls of Constantinople in June 1203. The Emperor Alexius III had made no preparation for their arrival; on the other hand, his nephew and namesake had led the Crusaders to believe that the city would open its gates in his support. It did not. To their chagrin they found their way barred. Whereupon the young pretender deserted his allies and crossed over into Asia. In the meantime his blind father, the ex-Emperor Isaac, was produced: the young Alexius was persuaded to return, and both father and son were proclaimed co-Emperors on August 1 1203 following another palace revolution and in the presence of the Crusader barons.

Alexius IV found it hard to fulfil the promises he had so rashly made to the Crusaders. In particular he failed to raise the money he said he would give them in return for their support. He partly solved this problem by melting down church plate and levying huge taxes on his political opponents. Consequently, he not only antagonised his subjects but failed to live up to the expectations of his allies. This only served to increase the suspicions of the latter, especially when they found that he was quite unable to control his government or to carry out any of his pledges. Within the city matters went from bad to worse, culminating in the murder of the co-Emperors in February 1204. This was regarded by the Crusaders as a direct challenge, and they thereupon decided to instal a westerner to succeed the murdered Emperors. With the help of traitors paid with Venetian money they successfully attacked and finally took the city on April 12 1204.

Once the chaos that followed the capture of the city had subsided, the Crusaders set about choosing a new Emperor. Boniface de Montferrat hoped to be chosen, and in order to enhance his chances he rescued the half-French, half-Hungarian ex-Empress Mary-Margaret and promptly married her. But the Venetians refused to accept him, insisting on a less powerful prince, Baldwin of Flanders, who was crowned in Saint Sofia on May 16 1204.

What happened to the Mandylion and the Keramion in the confusion following the entry of the Crusaders on April 12 1204 I shall discuss later. In a word, they disappeared along with many other relics, some of which subsequently came to light in France and elsewhere. This, then, was the starting point of my renewed quest for the Holy Grail.

# PART THREE
*The Wandering Shroud*

# FIVE

IN SEPTEMBER 1356, Jeanne de Vergy received the news of the death of her husband, Geoffrey de Charny, at the Battle of Poitiers. As Porte-Oriflamme, or Standard-Bearer of France, he had died gallantly defending his king against the attacking English. He was about fifty-six years old, and she was a little over twenty. Three years earlier King John II of France had granted Geoffrey a rent for the foundation of a collegiate church at Lirey, a small village he owned in Champagne not far from Troyes. He had sought permission to build it so that he might instal there the Holy Shroud of Christ, and on May 28, 1356 it had been solemnly inaugurated in the presence of Henri de Poitiers, Bishop of Troyes, the uncle of his future daughter-in-law. The Shroud was no longer in its golden, latticework casket, but instead a new one had been made for it, in which it remained until after 1453, when Marguerite de Charny, Geoffrey's grand-daughter, sold it to her kinsman, Louis, Duke of Savoy. Louis took it eventually to Chambéry, where it was kept in a silver casket, and from there his descendants took it to Turin, where it remains to this day. Following the death of the late King Umberto of Italy in March 1983, the Shroud passed out of the ownership of the House of Savoy into that of the Pope. How it came into the possession of the de Charny family was the next question I had to answer.

I began by tracing the family's ancestry, and soon discovered that they were a junior branch of the family of Mont-Saint-Jean, itself descended from the de Vergy family.

The earliest recorded seigneur de Mont-Saint-Jean was
Gollut, who claimed descent from Manassés, the founder of
the great castle of Vergy about 880. Nothing now remains of
this once impregnable fortress, which crowned the whole of
the summit of an isolated hill some three hundred metres long
about 17km south of Dijon, where it dominated the country
above the famous vineyards of Clos de Vougeot, Gevrey-
Chambertin and Vosne-Romanée. King Louis VII regarded it
as so strong that he offered it in 1159 to Pope Alexander III as
a refuge against the Emperor Frederick Barbarossa. Some
years earlier, Hugues II Sire de Mont-Saint-Jean, de Charny
and de Salmaise married his kinswoman, Elisabeth de Vergy,
by whom he had five sons and two daughters. Hugues was
generally recognised as so wise, pious and powerful a
nobleman that Popes Eugene III and Anastasius IV conferred
in 1149 and 1153 the rights and liberties of the great abbey of
Vezelay upon him in preference to the Count of Nevers. On
his death, in 1196, he was buried in the abbey of Cîteaux.

Etienne de Mont-Saint-Jean, Hugues' eldest son died
without issue two years after his father, in 1198, and was
succeeded by his brother, Guillaume. Among the many castles
and domains he inherited was Thoisy-le-Désert, 11km south-
east of his principal seat of Mont-Saint-Jean. In 1216 the
Templars were given lands at Thoisy, and in the course of the
next century they acquired a great deal more. By the middle of
the thirteenth century Thoisy-le-Désert had become one of
their most important preceptories in Burgundy.

Ponce, Hugues de Mont-Saint-Jean's third son, inherited
the seigneurie of Charny, a dependancy of the barony of
Mont-Saint-Jean, lying about 5km to the north, where the
family had built another strong castle.* He was the great-
grandfather of Geoffrey de Charny, the Porte-Oriflamme.
Etienne, Ponce and their sister Agnes had each married
members of the de Noyers family and their father-in-law,
Clérambault de Noyers had married Alix de Brienne, a great-
niece of King Louis VII and a sister of Jean de Brienne, King
of Jerusalem. Through these marriages, therefore, Geoffrey de
Charny was not only of royal descent, but a member of one of

---

*NOTE: See Genealogical Table I.

the four most powerful families in Burgundy. On his mother's side, he was descended from the de Joinvilles. She was Marguerite, the eldest daughter of Jean de Joinville, Hereditary Seneschal of Champagne and famous as the biographer of his king and close friend, St Louis. The de Joinvilles were also of royal descent and closely allied by marriage to the ruling houses of Champagne and Burgundy. Geoffrey de Charny's aunt, Alix de Joinville was the wife of Henry Plantagenet, Earl of Lancaster, a nephew of King Edward I of England. One of his great-uncles was Guillaume de Joinville, who while bishop of Langres bestowed large estates on the Templars of Burgundy. When he was translated to the archdiocese of Rheims, Guillaume de Joinville played an important part in bringing to an end the first part of the Albigensian Crusade. His support of the Templars can no doubt be attributed in some measure to the fact that one of his brothers, André de Joinville, was a member of the Order and Preceptor of Payns, just outside Troyes. Many of Geoffrey de Charny's ancestors and kinsmen had taken part in the Crusades.

Jeanne de Vergy came from an equally influential and aristocratic background, and she was, moreover, several times related to her husband. Her great-aunt, Alix de Vergy, had been Duchess of Burgundy and by all accounts a most remarkable woman.

In 1183 a quarrel arose between the reigning Duke of Burgundy, Hugh III, and Hugues de Vergy, which resulted first in civil war and ultimately in the surrender of the castle of Vergy to the Crown. The castle and barony were reunited to the duchy of Burgundy in 1199, however, by the marriage of Duke Odo III to Alix de Vergy. During this conflict Hugues de Vergy had been supported by his Mont-Saint-Jean kinsmen, but part of the settlement imposed by King Philippe-Augustus in 1185 on Hugues de Vergy and his father, Guy, included a substantial donation to the abbey of Cîteaux and the obligation to go on a Crusade. Both of these entailed raising money, which Hugues and his father obtained from the Templars. A document signed by Guy de Vergy in Acre in 1191 is part of these transactions. In it Guy grants the Templars a domain at Autrey, 45km northeast of Dijon for three years. In 1197 Hugues de Vergy gave his domain of Avosne, 20km north-east of Mont-Saint-Jean to the Templars.

When Hugues II de Mont-Saint-Jean and his wife, Elisabeth de Vergy, both died in 1196 a dispute arose concerning the inheritance of half the seigneurie of Vergy, of which she had been the owner as sole heiress of her father, Hervé de Vergy. Duke Odo III (who had not at that time married Alix de Vergy) took the part of Etienne de Mont-Saint-Jean, whom he appointed Seneschal of Burgundy. When Etienne died two years later, the Duke conferred the office on his brother, Guillaume de Mont-Saint-Jean. Thus on the eve of the Fourth Crusade, Alix de Vergy was Duchess of Burgundy and guillaume de Mont-Saint-Jean was Seneschal. They were thus among the few who knew all there was to know about the relics in Constantinople, and there seems little doubt that some members of either the de Vergy or Mont-Saint-Jean family must have seen the Mandylion in the course of the Second or Third Crusades. But how did they come to own it? The answer seemed to lie in the history of the Templars in Burgundy.

The Order was divided into eight "Langues" or tongues according to the languages of the particular areas. These were called Grand Priories and were directly subordinate to the Grand Master of the Order. They were, in order of seniority, Provence, Auvergne, France, Italy, Aragon (including Navarre, Catalonia, Roussillon and Sardinia), England (including Scotland and Ireland), Upper and Lower Germany (including Hungary, Bohemia, Poland, Denmark and Sweden), and Castile (including Leon, Portugal, Algarve, Granada, Toledo, Galicia and Andalusia). The headquarters of the Grand Prior of Provence was first at St Gilles and then at Montpellier, with a secondary headquarters at Toulouse. It was divided into fifty-four commanderies. Auvergne consisted of seventy-seven commanderies including Dôle and several houses in Burgundy to the east of Dijon. France was divided into a number of Priories of which the most important were those of Champagne, Burgundy, Aquitaine and Normandy, with important Temples at Troyes, Auxerre, Rheims, Sens and Etampes. Among these, however, the Priory of Champagne held a predominant position, for the Prior always held the office of Treasurer and Keeper of the Great Seal of the Order.

Each Grand Priory was divided into Priories, Preceptories, Sub-preceptories, Commanderies, "Membres" and "Granges". Because the Order was founded by men from Champagne, it is not surprising to find that the first Templar house in neighbouring Burgundy was founded at Bure-les-Templiers within ten years of its establishment, but from 1163 following the gift of the two adjoining villages of Leuglay and Voulaines by the Bishop of Langres, the seat of the Grand Prior of Champagne was moved to the latter, although this village was part of Burgundy. The Priory of Champagne soon became the most important in France, if not in Europe, and comprised twenty-four preceptories not just in Champagne and Burgundy but also in the dioceses of Metz, Nancy and Trier, ranking in importance with the eight Grand Priories. In 1175, Duke Hugh III of Burgundy gave money for the Order to build a castle at Voulaines, and further lands were added by the bishops of Langres (one of whom was Guillaume de Joinville) in 1208 and 1237. The castle, most of which has long since vanished, was strongly fortified, and is said to have contained a large chapter house whose walls were hung with the portraits of the Grand Masters.

A number of chapels were built in the surrounding forests among them those at Froidvent and Lugny on the road to Dijon and at Chapelle-du-Bois near the road from Voulaines to Val-des-Choues. Even today the neighbourhood of Voulaines and Leuglay is full of traces of the Templars' presence. In the woods round Essarois to the south as well as in the Bois-aux-Moines to the north can be found traces of crosses erected by the Order. It was in a cave near Essarois in 1789 that a discovery was made which helped, indirectly, to create the myth that the Templar "heresy" was akin to that of the Cathars. A small stone chest, no larger than a tea-caddy, embellished with strange bas reliefs and Arabic inscriptions was dug up by some workmen. In due course it came into the possession of the duc de Blacas, an amateur antiquarian, and eventually of the British Museum. Unfortunately it is an obvious 18th century fake, though it stimulated a great deal of interest at the time among those who wished to link the

Rosicrucians and Freemasons to the Templars.*

By now I had established without doubt close links between the de Vergy and de Charny families on the one hand and the Templars on the other. It remained for me to re-create the events which took place on the night of April 12/13, 1204 in Constantinople, and to find out what happened subsequently to see if they might throw light on the one-hundred-and-fifty-year disappearance of the Shroud. The unravelling of this mystery led me down some unexpected historical by-ways.

The first question I had to answer was this: How did the Mandylion and Keramion disappear from Constantinople in the course of the pillaging and looting that took place on that fateful night and during the following horrendous days, in the course of which more treasures of antiquity were lost than if there had been a major earthquake? Robert de Clari has no doubt about the matter, for he states quite categorically that they were not seen again by any Greek or Frenchman. The evidence is circumstantial, but the absence of reliable documentation certainly suggests that de Clari was right. Several possible relics were known to have existed, or even still to exist, in Paris, Genoa and Rome, but none of these can claim with such authority to have been the Mandylion as the Shroud of Turin.

The strongest reason for believing de Clari rests in the knowledge that the Pharos Treasury escaped the looting suffered elsewhere. Its relic collection was catalogued soon after the sack by Garnier de Trainel, Bishop of Troyes, and this has survived. His list contains nothing remotely like the Mandylion/Shroud. Robert de Clari, however, is emphatic that he saw the 'sydoine' at the church of St Mary of Blachernae. This suggests that it might have been taken there during the siege to be used as a talisman to protect the city in the same way that it had been used to protect Edessa from the Persians. The Crusaders' attack was against the Blachernae area, which was the first to be taken, and unlike the Pharos, it was not spared from looting. Consequently it could have been destroyed, and this is what most Byzantine scholars believe.

---

*See Appendix.

But that did not seem to be the end of the matter. The similarities between the Shroud and the Mandylion seemed to me to be the strongest evidence for believing in its escape, and modern scientific tests on the Shroud strongly support me. Permission for the temporary removal of the Mandylion from the Pharos to the Blachernae could only have been given by the highest authority in the City, namely the Emperor or the Patriarch. Until the beginning of April when the Crusaders first attacked, there would have been no reason to seek this permission, consequently the events leading up to the onslaught had to be examined in great detail.

Following the deaths of the co-Emperors, Isaac and Alexius IV, in February 1204, Alexius Murzuphlus was elected to succeed them as Alexius V. He was a vigorous but unpopular ruler, who attempted to organise the population in the defence of the city. He was unsuccessful. The first attack took place on April 6 and was repulsed with heavy losses. Six days later it was renewed, this time against the Blachernae, and was successful. Murzuphlus fled with his wife into Thrace. When this was known, the remaining nobles met in Saint Sofia to offer the crown to Theodore Lascaris, who refused it. Together with his family, the Patriarch and many of the nobility, he fled across the Boshporus and took refuge in Asia. There is no evidence that any of these took the Mandylion or any other relics with them. By next morning, April 13, the Doge of Venice and the leading Crusaders rode through the city from the Blachernae to occupy the Boukoleon Palace. There they found several high-ranking ladies sheltering in it, including Agnes, the sister of the King of France, who had been the wife of Alexius IV, and was now the wife of a Byzantine nobleman, Theodore Vrancas, and the ex-Empress Mary-Margaret. The latter, following the flight of the Patriarch and the Emperor Alexius Murzuphlus, was the only person in authority to remain in the city during that terrible two days and nights.

It is most unlikely that the Mandylion would have left the Pharos Treasury in the Boukoleon Palace before the beginning of April – probably not until it was clear that the Crusaders were intending to attack the city, say about April 1. Following the rebuff of April 6 – attributed no doubt to the relic's efficacy – it would probably have been returned to its usual resting place. When the attack was renewed on April 12 it might have been brought out again, but sometime during the night of April 12/13 it disappeared. Once the Patriarch and Emperor had fled, the way was open for Agnes Vrancas or the ex-Empress Mary-Margaret to take possession of it. They alone remained, the widows of two recent Emperors; they alone were predisposed to support the Crusaders, many of whom were their close kinsfolk. After what the Byzantines had done to her husband and step-son, the ex-Empress Mary-Margaret cannot have had much love for them.

And so, I argued, if the Mandylion, and maybe also the Keramion, survived, as I believe the former certainly did, it must have come into the hands of someone influential enough and rich enough to withstand the temptation to sell it on the relic market, where it would have fetched a king's ransom. The most likely was one of the ex-Empresses, and of these, Mary-Margaret, as the widow of the most recent, would have been the senior, more especially as the Princess Agnes was now the wife of a mere nobleman.

The ex-Empress Mary-Margaret was the daughter of King Bela III of Hungary by his first wife, Agnes de Chatillon, and the step-daughter of Marguerite de France, King Bela's second wife, the daughter of King Louis VII of France and widow of Henry Courtmantel, the "Young King" and eldest son of King Henry II of England.* Mary-Margaret was born about 1175 and had married the Emperor Isaac when she was ten. She was consequently still a young woman of under thirty when she found herself in lonely charge of the Boukoleon Palace on the night of April 12/13. Boniface de Montferrat received the surrender of the Palace, and almost at once proposed to marry the young ex-Empress. The wedding took place before the end of April 1204, and through this he hoped to be elected Emperor by his fellow Crusaders. He was not. By way of consolation he was offered and accepted the throne of Salonica, a Kingdom which then included parts of Thrace, Macedonia and northern Greece. Boniface and Mary-Margaret left Constantinople in July 1204 and took up

*See Genealogical Table II.

# TABLE OF DESCENT OF MARGUERITE DE CHARNY

Dame de Montfort, de Savoisy, de Lirey
from the Kings of France.

Source: Pere Anselme 'Histoire de la
Maison Royale de France'

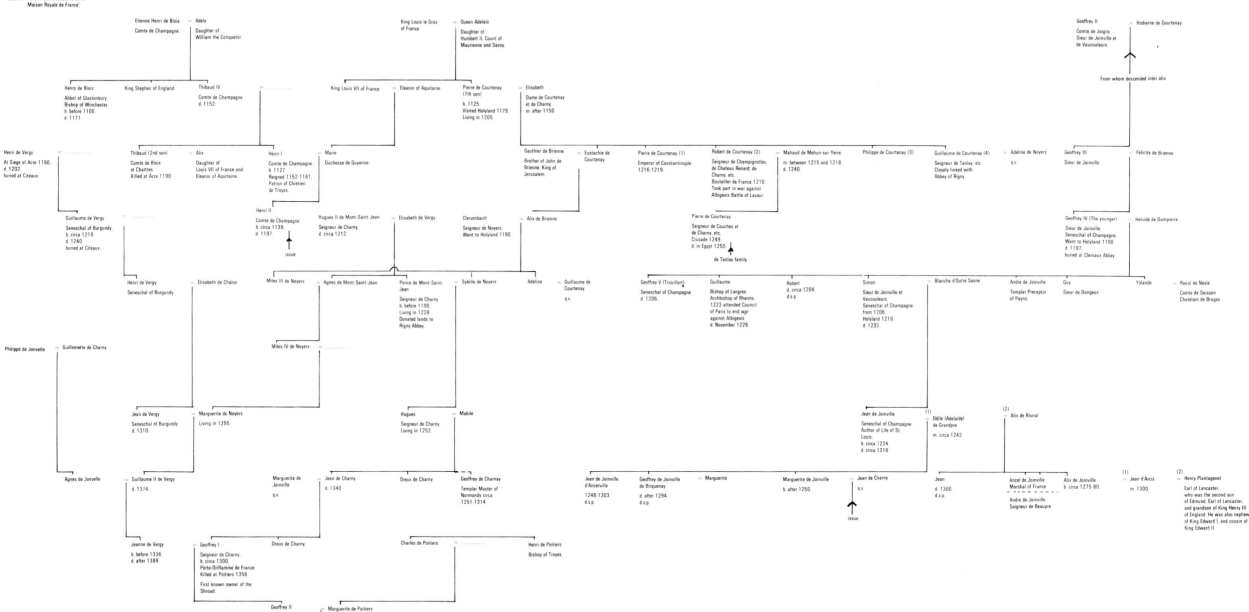

residence in their new kingdom in September. It is clear from the account of an eyewitness, Geoffrey de Villehardouin, that they took much of the imperial treasure with them, for Boniface was compelled to return the imperial vestments and vermilion boots to the new Emperor, Baldwin, in November 1204. Among those who were also eyewitnesses to these events was Geoffrey de Charny's great-grandfather, the man after whom he was named, Geoffrey de Joinville, Seneschal of Champagne. Did they take the Mandylion as well?

Mary-Margaret's marriage to Boniface did not last long, for he died in the early summer of 1207. In the meantime she had borne him a son, Demetrios, who became King of Salonica in succession to his father, and who was crowned on January 6, 1208. Mary-Margaret's second widowhood was shorter than her first. Within a year of Boniface's death she married Nicholas de Saint-Omer, a son of the titular prince of Galilee and a kinsman of Godfrey de Saint-Omer, one of the two founders of the Order of Knights Templar. This marriage lasted little longer than the last for Nicholas died in 1212, but not before Mary-Margaret had borne him two sons, Bela and William de Saint-Omer. Ten years later in 1222, Mary-Margaret was driven into exile following the collapse of the kingdom of Salonica, which she had ruled as regent for her son, Demetrios. She took refuge with her three surviving sons in Hungary at the Court of her brother King Andrew II. He appointed her eldest son, Kalojan, (whom she had had by the Emperor Isaac) Duke of Sirmium. This province had originally been Margaret's dowry when she married the Emperor, and she was appointed regent on his behalf.

The reign of Margaret's father, Bela III (1172-1196) was a glorious period in the history of Hungary. His family relations assured him a high place in the hierarchy of European monarchs, and was consequently a reason for making me believe that he would have been aware of the nature and extent of the collection of relics at Constantinople. During his reign French influence in Hungary reached its highest point. His two French queens brought with them knights, priests and architects from France. French literary influence on Hungary was extensive, and knowledge of the popular romances, including those of Chrétien de Troyes and Robert

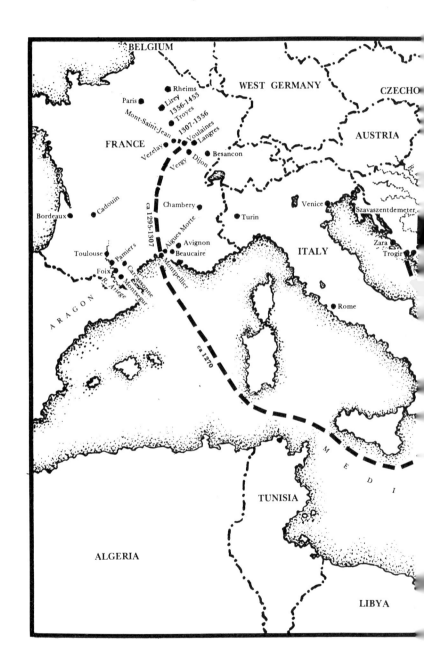

de Boron spread rapidly at Court and among the nobility. During the reigns of Bela III's successors, Imre (1196-1204) and Andrew II (1205-1235), at least two Pronvençal troubadours, Pierre Vidal and Gaucelm Faidit, are known to have turned up at the Court of Esztergom, then the capital of the country. In church matters French influence was equally strong. Bela III invited the Cistercians to Hungary and granted them considerable privileges. In the reign of his feckless son, Andrew II, huge estates were given to this and other religious orders, including the Templars and Knights of St John of Jerusalem.

Bela III was succeeded by his eldest son, Imre, and by Imre's son, Ladislas III, who between them reigned only nine years. They were succeeded in turn by Bela's second son, Andrew II in 1205. He was an incompetent spendthrift, who conducted fourteen unsuccessful wars of agression in the first fifteen years of his reign. Nevertheless, he managed to maintain peaceful relations with his two most powerful neighbours, the Emperor of Byzantium and the Holy Roman Emperor.

Having put off for twenty-two years the vow originally taken by his father to lead a Crusade, he decided in 1217 to join the Fifth Crusade. By this time Hungary's finances were so weakened by the king's bad management that large-scale borrowings had to be made. Andrew turned to the Jews for help, but even so he was compelled to sell Zara in Dalmatia to the Republic of Venice in order to pay them for the transport of his troops to the Holy Land.

In 1215, Andrew married Yolande de Courtenay, the daughter of Peter de Courtenay, who two years later become Latin Emperor of Constantinople. By this marriage he became an uncle by marriage of Alix de Brienne, the wife of Clérambault de Noyers.* During his absence in Palestine, Andrew appointed two regents for his infant son, the future Bela IV. One of these was the French Archbishop of Esztergom and the other an Italian Templar named Poncio della Croce. The former was appointed to rule over the northern provinces of the kingdom, the latter over Dalmatia

---

*See Genealogical Table I.

and Croatia. This campaign brought Hungary to the very brink of bankruptcy, and nothing was achieved beyond the acquisition of two doubtful relics, one of them the water-jug used at the marriage feast of Cana, the other the head of St Stephen.

Andrew's inefficiency both as a soldier and as a statesman and financier bordered on lunacy: it once happened that he granted the same estate to two different people. He made over huge tracts of land in perpetuity, whereby the beneficiaries got it in full ownershop without any obligations attached. The consequent decline in his income was not compensated from other sources. Luckily Andrew was not long in Palestine, for within a few weeks of his arrival he decided to return home. This time he travelled overland, calling on the way at Constantinople to visit his father-in-law, the Emperor, Peter de Courtenay. From here his most direct way home lay through his sister's kingdom of Salonica. I could not find out for certain whether he took this route, but it would be surprising if he had not, for the only other one lay through the territory of the Bulgarian King who was not well-disposed towards him. Andrew arrived back in Hungary by the end of 1218.

The year 1222 not only saw the return of Mary-Margaret to her native land, but also the signature by her brother of the Golden Bull, Hungary's Magna Carta. Under it the power of the king and the church were severely curtailed, much to the displeasure of the Pope and the Hungarian bishops and clergy. From this time onward the latter began to support the "Young King", Bela IV, who had been crowned prior to his father's departure for the Holy Land.

Bela IV was everything his father was not. Both while he was Crown Prince (or more properly Young King) and after his accession in 1235, he did everything he could to bolster the royal power and to recover the lands his father had so rashly given away or mortgaged. His constant aim was to get the better of the Jewish moneylenders, who had acquired not only crown lands as security for their loans, but also commercial benefits of all kinds. One of his first acts as King was to re-establish the central power of the crown and to revise the donations his father had bestowed in excessive quantities on the church, especially on convents belonging to the

Cistercians and Knights of the Hospital of St John.

Dr Csocsán de Várallja points out that Andrew II was a member of the latter Order, from whom he undoubtedly obtained financial and military support. There is no evidence to suggest that *he* sold or pawned the Shroud to them. Apart from anything else, it did not belong to him. His son, Bela IV, on the other hand, had an equally close relationship with the Templars, and since the two Orders were often at odds with one another, it seems likely that it was through Bela's agency, rather than his father's that the Shroud passed into their hands.

In 1241 the Tatars invaded Hungary, forcing Bela IV and the Hungarian royal family to seek refuge in the Templar stronghold of Klis, a few miles inland from the Dalmatian city of Split. They had suffered great hardship during the invasion, and at one stage Bela IV had been forced to take refuge in Austria, where, like Richard Coeur de Lion some sixty years before, he was kept in restraint until a ransom was paid for his release. During 1241 and 1242 there had been hardly any possibility to gather in the harvest, and the country was consequently starving. Bela had been able to rescue the Crown of St Stephen and other crown jewels, together with what remained in the Treasury, only with the greatest difficulty, and had ordered his queen, Mary Lascaris, to take them to Klis.

In the spring of 1242 an epidemic broke out in the wake of the invaders. This killed Bela's two eldest daughters, Catherine and Margaret (the latter had recently married her cousin, William de Saint-Omer, the younger son of the ex-Empress Mary-Margaret). The two princesses were buried in the cathedral of Split, and when William himself died in April 1242, he was buried in the Collegiate Church of nearby Trogir. His tomb has disappeared, but the epitaph that once adorned it was copied and has survived. I shall quote it in full, for it is a critical piece of evidence in our story of the wandering Shroud.

*Jacet hoc sub lapide nobilis Gulielmus*
*Jacet heros inclitus operit quem tellus*
*Nepos Belle Tertii regis Ungarorum*
*Margarite genitus Domine Grecorum*
*Dicti regis filie Grecis Dominatrix*

*Constantinopoleos sceptris Imperatrix*
*Arcente denique barbaro perverso*
*Infinitis Tartaris Marte sub adverso*
*Quartum Bella prosequens ejus consorbrinum*
*Ad mare prevenerat usque Dalmatinum*
*Ubi ad comercia vitae celsioris*
*Mortis solvit debitum jussu creatoris*
*Anni Christi fluxerant mille cum ducentis*
*Quadraginta duo plus computo legentis*
*Aprilis vigesima die jam transacta*
*Qua Gulielmi spiritus reddidit ad astra*
*Heu accedit inclita sponsa Margarita*
*Sanctum gerens spiritum moribus et vita*
*Nam cuncta quae moriens ita vir legavit*
*Dispergens pauperibus prorsus erogavit*
*Qualia ecclesiae tulit ornamenta*
*Ex imperialibus pannis vestimenta*
*Patent intuentibus lucem et supernam*
*Ejus postulent requiem eternam.*

Roughly translated this means: Here lies the noble prince William, grandson of Bela III, King of the Hungarians, by Margaret, his daughter, Queen of the Greeks and Empress of Constantinople, who flying from the invading Tatars followed Bela IV in his adversity to the coasts of Dalmatia, where he died on April 20 1242. The said William gave up the ghost along with his consort, Margaret, and at his death he bequeathed to the poor the cloth and other imperial vestments he had removed from the Imperial Treasury, which gave to those who look upon it eternal rest from on high."

The most curious passage is that which speaks of William's bequest to the poor of a cloth from Constantinople which gives light and eternal rest to those who gaze upon it. What else could this cloth be but the Shroud/Mandylion? But who were the poor to whom he gave such a valuable relic? Dr Csocsán de Várallja is of the opinion, and I agree with him, that they were not the multitude, but his poor relations, the Hungarian Royal family.

I have recounted this period of Hungarian history very briefly,

but the more I considered it, the more I felt that the clue to the
whereabouts of the Shroud rested in the doings of the ex-
Empress Mary-Margaret, for she provides the link between
Constantinople, Hungary and the Templars. I became convinced that if anyone had had an opportunity and the motive
to take it, it was she. This did not, of course, explain how it
came into the hands of the de Vergy and de Charny families,
but at least I seemed to have taken a step forward in time.

Let us look at this a little more closely. Prince William and
his wife, Princess Margaret, Bela IV's second daughter, had
had a daughter of their own, also called Margaret, who was
then an infant of but a few months old. At the age of 9 she was
sent to join her aunt, yet another Margaret, (the future Saint
Margaret of Hungary) in a Dominican convent, where she
lived until 1276. Consequently, William's next of kin would
have been his father-in-law, King Bela IV if we ignore his
youngest brother, Bela de Saint-Omer, of whom I shall have
something to say in a moment.

Bela IV's only financial assets at this time consisted of the
Hungarian Crown Jewels, which he could not dispose of for
obvious reasons. His only hope was to borrow money from the
Templars, in whose castle he and his family had taken refuge.
The Templars, however, were then the bankers of Europe;
they were also hard-headed businessmen, and always
demanded security for the money they lent. It would have
been essential, therefore, for Bela IV to offer them something
of value by way of security: could this have been the Shroud/
Mandylion?

In the city of Salonica there is a very ancient church dating
from the ninth or tenth century. It was originally called the
Basilica of the Theotokos, which means the Church of the
Mother of God. During the Turkish occupation of Salonica it
was turned into a mosque and is now in a considerable state of
disrepair. Nevertheless, the only royal person known to have
been associated with it in the middle ages was Marie de Montferrat, who, of course, was none other than the ex-Empress
Mary-Margaret. Furthermore, at some period of its history its
name was changed from Theotokos to Hagia Paraskevi or
Akheiropoeitos, which mean Good Friday and Not-made-by-
human-hands respectively. Now this struck me as highly

significant, not only because, as I have shown the Mandylion was so intimately connected with Good Friday when it was in Constantinople, but also the term Akheiropoeitos was often used in connection with sindon of Christ, the Mandylion. This strikes me as a piece of strongly circumstantial evidence to support the theory that the ex-Empress did take the Mandylion with her when she went to Salonica. If that were the case, then it was likely that she also took it to Hungary when she left that city in 1222.

From 1208 to 1222 Mary-Margaret was compelled to spend large sums of money to support her young son's kingdom. If she were the owner of the Shroud she could have raised a very large loan on the security of it. If she had done so, several things might have happened; either the Shroud would have passed directly into the hands of the lender, or it might have stayed in the custody of a third party mutually agreeable to the ex-Empress and her creditors such as the clergy of the Basilica of Theotokos. As I've already pointed out, the only bankers rich enough to finance such a loan were the Templars, and because her third husband's family had been so closely associated with the Order from the time of its foundation, they were the obvious people to turn to. However, even if Mary-Margaret did not need such a substantial sum of money, her impoverished nephew certainly did. It is uncertain when she died, but it was after 1229, which is the date of the last known reference to her in historical records.

Of one thing we can be reasonably certain. Having taken the relic from Constantinople in 1204 it is highly unlikely that Mary-Margaret or her sons would have left it behind in Salonica when they went to Hungary in 1222. Perhaps, I thought, I might find a clue to this by studying the Templar's banking methods.

In 1240, for example, the Latin Emperor, Baldwin II, mortgaged the True Cross as guarantee for a large sum of money he borrowed from the Templars of Syria. Two years earlier he had gone to Paris where he sold the Crown of Thorns to Louis IX. The fact that there was already one in the cathedral of St Denis doesn't seem to have disturbed anyone unduly. On the contrary, Louis IX (better known as Saint Louis) built the Sainte Chapelle expressly to house this new one. Both crowns disappeared in the French Revolution.

The Order's banking activities were confined to four fields: loans, advances and bonds; payments over long distances and the transmission of funds generally; the recovery of debts; and payments on current account. Templar treasuries were universally regarded as safe places to keep money and valuables against payments which had to be made as the result of treaties, marriage contracts and all kinds of public and private agreements. These capital sums, coupled with the deeds of land and property, formed the basis of the Order's legendary wealth. Every major preceptory was thus a local treasury offering a service not so very different from a modern bank. Indeed, it is said that the Templars invented cheques. In the case of doubtful creditors, guarantees were always required, and money, gold, silver or other valuables equivalent in value to the sum borrowed had to be deposited in return for cash

The case of Pierre Desde and his wife, for example, is a typical one. They borrowed money to go on a pilgrimage to the Holy Land in 1135. In order to pay for their trip they gave the Order in Saragossa in Spain their houses, lands and other property. In return the Templars gave them (out of charity so as not to infringe the Church's law against usury) enough money for their journey. While they were away, the brethren kept the income from the estate and when the pilgrims returned, they were allowed to live on their land for the rest of their lives and to use the income for themselves. On the death of the survivor, all the property reverted to the Order for ever. This practice had the double effect of vastly increasing the landed holdings of the Order, and of causing much ill-feeling on the part of the heirs who found themselves done out of their inheritance.

Mary-Margaret bequeathed the Dukedom of Sirmium to her eldest son, Kalojan, where he reigned from 1235 to 1254. In the latter year, he was succeeded by Prince Ratislav of Chernigov, who had married Princess Anna, Bela IV's third daughter, though he was still living in 1259. There is good reason for believing that Kalojan continued to adhere to the Orthodox Church, though his mother, once she returned to her native country, reverted to the Roman Catholic faith. She

even went so far as to try to supplant the Byzantine rite in
Sirmium while she ruled it. Consequently, she would have
been unlikely to leave a relic as holy as the Mandylion to
Kalojan, but rather to her Frankish, Catholic son, William de
Saint-Omer. In fact, this is all she did leave him, for she left
her youngest son, Bela de Saint-Omer her Greek estates near
Thebes.

King Bela IV, unlike his father, was a staunch friend of the
Templars. He not only confirmed such grants of land as his
father had made to them, but he looked to them for support
when his kingdom was attacked by the Tatars in 1241.
Warnings of this impending catastrophe were sounded as
early as 1238, but when the Asiatic hordes eventually broke
through the Carpathian passes into the broad Hungarian
plain, Bela was deserted by most of his barons, who resented
his attempt to claw back to the crown some of the lands his
father had so unthinkingly distributed among them. The
Templars alone came to his rescue and remained loyal to him.
The king was forced to retreat to Croatia and then down the
Dalmatian coast with the remnants of his army, which largely
consisted of Templars and priests. He reached Zagreb some
50km from Szavaszentdemeter where, perhaps, the Shroud
was then kept, in 1242 bringing with him the relics his father
had brought from the Holy Land in 1217 and whatever else of
value they could carry. He sent his queen and their children
ahead to Split, where they stayed only a few days before
taking refuge in the Templar stronghold of Klis. Bela IV, with
the Tatars on his heels, eventually reached Split, intent on
escaping by sea to one of the many offshore islands. There
were no ships to take him and his army of priests and knights,
so he moved his wife and all his treasure to Trogir a few miles
up the coast. The Tatar attack on Split was repulsed, but after
a few days the enemy advanced on Trogir. This city is built on
a small island linked to the mainland by a bridge, which the
Hungarians were able to destroy. The Tatars had no boats to
cross the narrow stretch of water, so they laid siege to the city
from the landward side only. Within a few days, news came to
the Tatar commander of the death of the Great Khan and as
rapidly as they had come, the Asiatic horde withdrew
southward and then east into Bulgaria and the southern

Trogir                                                    Yugoslav Travel Agency

steppes of Russia. By the middle of 1242 the evacuation of Hungary was complete, but the devastation left behind was appalling.

No sooner had the Tatars departed than Bela IV began rebuilding his kingdom. The queen, however, remained in Klis another year. If it had not already done so, the Shroud must by now have passed into the hands of the Templars, who alone were able and willing to help the king restore his shattered kingdom. Had it remained the property of the Hungarian royal family, it seems inconceivable to me that there should be no record of the fact. After careful examination of as many contemporary records as I could find, short of going to Hungary itself, I felt convinced that I could put a date beyond which the Shroud no longer remained in the Balkans.

What probably happened was this: following the sack of Constantinople in April 1204, the Mandylion and perhaps the Keramion and other relics, too, fell into the hands of Mary-Margaret and her husband, Boniface. They took them to Salonica, where they remained until she was forced to leave in 1222, unless her brother Andrew II, persuaded her to let him take them to Hungary when he returned from the Holy Land in 1218 with his water-jar from Cana and head of Saint Stephen. At all events, they were probably taken to Szavas-zentdemeter until such time as they were removed by William de Saint-Omer, who may have inherited them at his mother's death sometime around 1230, or they may have been among the treasures brought by the royal family from Esztergom and Székesfehérvár when they fled before the Tatars, and took refuge with the Templars at Klis.

It seems to me that the most likely date for the transfer to the Templars was 1242. In that year Bela IV was compelled to raise money to rehabilitate his ruined country, and William de Saint-Omer's epitaph at Trogir lends support to the belief that it was he and his mother who had brought the Mandylion from Constantinople, and left it to his impoverished kinsfolk, who mortgaged or sold it to the Templars.

Finally, William de Saint-Omer had large estates in southern Italy, where he had spent a good deal of time between 1222, when he left Salonica before his marriage to Bela's daughter in 1230. This could account for the presence in Bari of the icon which Jacques Pantaléon bought for his sister in Laon. It has also to be remembered that Godfrey de Saint-Omer, one of William's collateral ancestors, was among the eight or so founding knights of the Order of Templars, and that his family's links with the Order had remained firm. There is no evidence that the Angelos dynasty, to which Kalojan belonged, was in any way connected with it.

Having traced the probable history of the Mandylion from 1204 to about 1230 or 1240, I had next to look at the romances to see what evidence I could find for believing that it did in fact come into the hands of the Templars. In order to do this, I had also to make up my mind about the Cathar treasure of Mont-ségur; what was its nature? when did it reach the castle? who brought it and when? what, if any connection was there between the Cathars and the Hungarian royal family? I decided to pursue my study of the Templars, and this, I found, yielded me exciting and valuable results.

# PART FOUR
*The Idol of the Templars*

# SIX

GEOFFREY ASHE and other Arthurian scholars say that the association of the Templars with the Grail is a "favoured guess". There is, it must be admitted, no direct evidence of the fact, although Wolfram does call the Grail knights "Templeisen", this may be by analogy only. All the same, both the *Parzival* and the *Perlesvaus* refer to the Grail being in the care of knightly hermits who wear red crosses on their robes. On initiation each Templar was given a white robe or mantle, later superimposed with a red cross symbolising the crucified body of Christ.

The Order was given the 'coup de grâce' in 1317, when the Pope, John XXII confirmed the provisional sentence of his predecessor Clement V. For nearly two centuries, the Templars had been councillors, diplomats and bankers for popes, emperors, kings and nobles. At the same time they had been valiant defenders of religious orthodoxy. The Order was founded in about 1119 by Godfrey de Saint-Ômer and Hugues de Payens for the protection of pilgrims visiting the Holy Land, and some ten years later at a Council held at Troyes, the Order had been given new rules, which insisted on the observation of poverty, chastity and obedience, the defence of the poor, of pilgrims and of Christian truth. These rules were inspired, if not written, by St Bernard, whose standing in Champagne and Burgundy was second to none. Arising from these rules, the Order developed a particular veneration for the Real Presence of Christ, which in time became a kind of

89

mystical theology of its own. But the chief purpose of the Order and the aim of every knight was to see the "unveiled countenance of the Lord Jesus", in return for which he was required to show unwavering courage and to practise total chastity.

Templar churches were different from others in having round naves in imitation of the Dome of the Rock or the Church of the Holy Sepulchre in Jerusalem (opinions differ about this). Being so deeply attached to Christ's earthly appearance, and his death so central to their thinking, once the existence of the Shroud became known it must have been the supreme desire of the Order to possess it. This matched the divine vision earmarked for the Templars by Saint Bernard. With the sack of Constantinople and the financial difficulties of the king of Hungary, the way was at last open for them to obtain it.

In spite of their valour and piety, the Templars acquired immense wealth, largely as a result of their banking activities, and with it great power. By the beginning of the fourteenth century they had almost become a state wthin a state in France, and this ultimately led to the Order's suppression by the King, Philip the Fair.

This king set out to achieve two objectives: to keep a strong hand on the influence of the Papacy in French affairs, and to consolidate his political power by seizing the wealth of the Templars, just as Henry VIII was to do in very different circumstances two hundred and fifty years later in England. The unexpected death of Pope Benedict XI gave him his chance. The Conclave to elect the late Pope's successor was evenly balanced and nine months slipped by without an election. Finally King Philip intervened and proposed his own nominee, Bertrand de Goth, Archbishop of Bordeaux, and a native of Languedoc, but not before he had interviewed him and laid down certain conditions for his support. Most, but not all these conditions are known, but there is good reason to believe that one of them was the assurance that if elected, Archbishop de Goth would agree to the dissolution of the Order of Knights Templar. De Goth was elected, and took the name of Clement V. Henceforth the king held the Papacy in his pocket, and made sure that it stayed there after the Pope had installed himself at Avignon.

In the spring of 1307 the King met the Pope at Poitiers, where the latter was compelled to agree to the overthrow of the Templars. Before agreeing to the King's request, Clement V played for time and demanded proof of the crimes with which the King was accusing them. These consisted of accusations of heresy, idolatry, sodomy and sundry other sins and misdemeanours. Such "proof" was cooked up and the Pope lent his support to the *coup d'état* which the King had planned for the following autumn. The great secretiveness of the Order gave rise to fantastic rumours, and these increased in number and became more and more fantastic in proportion to its ever increasing wealth and power. Inevitably the Templars became more and more unpopular, and the worst possible construction was put on any real or imagined scandal that might be attached to them. The most sensational of these was the accusation that the brethren worshipped a mysterious "Idol" or "Head", before which they would throw themselves down on the ground with shouts of "Yallah".

It shows how hostile public opinion towards the Templars had become that no one thought fit to ask whose "head" or image an Order of brethren so firmly dedicated to the defence of Christianity might be venerating. Many commentators have found this almost inexplicable, but I believe there is a very simple explanation. The source of most of our information comes from the interrogation of individual knights by the Inquisition, from which it is quite clear that only the most senior members of the Order attended ceremonies at which the "head" was exposed for worship. Of one thing we can be quite sure: statements given to the Inquisition in no way give the impression of being in any way false or designed to put the Inquisitors off the scent, in spite of the fact that they were almost invariably made after the knights had been subjected to the most frightful tortures. The evidence of a number of Burgundian Templars is therefore of great significance, because of the special nature of the Grand Priory of Voulaines. This seems to confirm the theory that the Shroud/Grail was taken there some time during the twenty years or so preceding the dissolution of the Order.

Brother Jean Taillefer, of the diocese of Langres, for

example, was received into the Order at Mormant, one of the three preceptories directly under the government of the Grand Priory of Voulaines (the others were at Epailly and Bure). He said that at his initiation "an idol representing a human face" was placed on the altar before him. Hugues de Bure, another Burgundian from the same diocese described how a "head" was taken out of a cupboard, or aumbry, in the chapel, and that it seemed to him to be of silver, copper or gold, and to represent a head with a long beard. This might well have been a description of an icon similar to the one at Laon, and because several Templars said there were a large number of copies of the "idol", and that these were customarily kept in chests or coffers, it is not unreasonable to assume that Hugues de Bure is describing one of them. Another brother said there were at least four of these copies in England. No doubt the painting found recently at Templecombe in Somerset was one of these.

Brother Pierre d'Arbley suspected that the "idol" had two faces, which may mean that some copies faithfully represented the frontal and dorsal images of the head on the Shroud. His kinsman, Guillaume d'Arbley, made the point that the "idol" itself, as distinct from copies of it, were only exhibited at General Chapters. His statement therefore indirectly confirms those of other Templars who said they had never seen the "idol" because they had never attended a General Chapter of the Order.

Brother Pierre-Regnier de Larchent, from the diocese of Sens, said that although he had never seen the "idol" he believed it was always kept in the custody of the Grand Master or the brother who presided over General Chapters. I find this particularly significant when it is remembered that the Grand Prior of Voulaines was ex-officio Treasurer of the Order, and that for the first ten years of his reign as Grand Master, Jaques de Molay was in Cyprus, England or Provence and did not take up residence in the Paris Temple until 1300.

Brother Jean-Denis de Taverniac said that Grand Master Guillaume de Beaujeu, whose term of office ran from 1273 to 1291, and after him, Hugues de Pairaud, who narrowly failed to be elected Grand Master in 1292, were the first to hold these special chapters at which the "idol" was exhibited.

The Treasurer of the Paris Temple, Brother Jean de Turn, spoke of a painted head in the form of a picture, which he had adored at one of these chapters. Since all who had attended them agreed unanimously they were held shortly before dawn, it is hardly surprising, given the dim nature of the lighting, that their descriptions of the holy object are somewhat vague. In the prevailing gloom it would have been very difficult to see the face on the Shroud, which even in broad daylight is fairly indistinct. But the timing of these ceremonies seems to me to be important, for it suggests that the rising of the sun was being linked symbolically with the body of Christ rising from the tomb. While such symbolism would have had immense significance for those in the secret of the Shroud, it is not hard to see why those who were not privy to it might have regarded it as heretical.

There is another aspect of the Templar initiation ceremony I find interesting in this context. When the moment came for the postulant to take his vows, he was required to place his hand, not on the Bible, but on a Missal open at the point in the Mass where the body of Christ is mentioned. Yet several priests attached to the Order, such as Bertrand de Villers and Étienne de Dijon, both from the diocese of Langres, stated that at this point in the Mass they were told to omit the words "Hoc est corpus meum". Could this be because in the presence of the Shroud they were all in the Real Presence of Christ's body, thus rendering the Host superfluous?

Finally, there is the apparently absurd accusation that the "idol" was a bearded woman. Nearly all the brethren agreed that the head was bearded and had long hair. This, of course, tallies with the head on the Shroud. The frontal image shows Christ's hair to be shoulder-length, and the dorsal image that he wore a pigtail. The fourteenth century was not alone in disapproving of men with long hair: we have witnessed in our own day the bitter hostility that such a hairstyle can arouse among more conservative elements of society. It is one of the more curious manifestations of prejudice that throughout the history of Europe (and more especially Catholic and Protestant Europe) there has only been one brief period, from about 1620 to 1750, when it has been socially acceptable to the establishment for men to wear very long hair. At all other

times long hair has been taken as a sign of effeminacy, protest
or subversiveness. Contemporary iconography depicted Jesus
in countless statues and pictures with fairly short hair, and it
was only in the Orthodox East, where even today priests wear
long hair and beards, that we find him thus depicted. To the
Inquisitors, therefore, the very idea that the Templars might
be worshipping a long-haired, bearded figure was highly
suspect, for it smacked of the blackest heresy almost amount-
ing to blasphemy. Regardless of any other crimes or misdemeanours they may have been suspected of, this was by far
the worst. On the other hand, believing as they did, that the
image on the Shroud revealed the true face of Christ, it is not
difficult to understand why the Templars might have rejected
the conventional iconography of Jesus.

Dr Malcolm Barber, in his comprehensive study of the trial
of the Templars lists the charges against the Order in 1308
under seven broad headings, of which the second consists of
the following items:

> That in each province they (the Order) had idols,
>     namely heads, of which some had three faces,
>     and some one, and others had a human skull.
>
> That they adored these idols or that idol, and
>     especially in their *great chapters and assemblies*. (My
>     italics)
>
> That they venerated (them).
>
> That (they venerated them) as God.
>
> That (they venerated them) as their Saviour.
>
> That some of them (did).
>
> That the majority of those who were in the
>     chapters (did).
>
> That they said that the head could save them.
>
> That (it could) make riches.
>
> That it gave them all the riches of the Order.
>
> That it made the trees flower.
>
> That (it made) the land germinate.
>
> That they surrounded or touched each head of the
>     aforesaid idols with small cords, which they wore
>     around themselves next to the shirt or the flesh.
>
> That in his reception, the aforesaid small cords or
>     some lengths of them were given to each of the

brethren.

That they did this in veneration of an idol.

That it was enjoined on them that they should wear the small cords around themselves and they did this even by night.

That they (the receptors) enjoined them (the postulants) on oath, that they should not reveal the aforesaid.

Dr Barber points out that the charges were not a random collection but an attempt "to play upon the deep-seated fears of contemporaries" in much the same way as accusations of witchcraft and heresy were levelled against certain groups in society in seventeenth century England and America. Some of the accusations, such as spitting on the cross, homosexuality, misappropriation of funds and the irregular absolution from sins were either total fabrications or deliberate misrepresentations of the Order's customs and practice designed to bolster the case against them.

The charges relating to the idol, although grotesque in many respects, can, nonetheless, be partially explained by reference to the Shroud, and deserve to be examined in this light. If, as the charges suggest, copies of the head of Christ, perhaps similar to the icon of Laon, were widely distributed throughout the Order's houses, this would explain why none of them, which must have come to light when the Order was arrested in 1307, even so much as caused a raised eyebrow. Some, indeed, may have been three-dimensional representations, but they cannot have been in any way out of the ordinary, otherwise the French government of Philip the Fair would have produced them as damning evidence against the Order, for it is inconceivable that all of them were hidden or destroyed before the king's men carried out the arrests on October 13, 1307.

Although these ceremonies were held at night and in the greatest secrecy, there is no evidence for believing that they were in any way heretical, but they may have differed in minor respects from those of other monastic orders. On the other hand, the very fact that they were surrounded by so much secrecy made everyone else highly suspicious of them. Here we find a striking difference between the Templars and the

Cathars. The latter went to their deaths in droves as martyrs for their beliefs, but there is no evidence whatever that the Templars did. They either died under torture, refusing to confess that they held any heretical beliefs, or, to put an end to unbearable pain, they 'confessed' to the sins of which they were accused and promptly and unreservedly asked to be forgiven. This strikes me as showing that far from being satanic, the Templar head was more likely to have been the divine likeness of Christ in a form which mortal men are not normally privileged to see. I was thus driven to the view that there is a strong case for believing that the Templar "Idol" was none other than the Mandylion with its true likeness of Christ not made by human hands.

It is not uncommon for hostile comment to throw light on the true nature of things. One accusation levelled at the Templars said that at their services the priest had nothing to do except recite Psalm 67. I found this a most revealing statement, for it provides a means of linking Templar with Grail ceremonial. One of the brethren said in evidence to the Inquisition that the "Idol" was the Saviour who makes the trees blossom and who ripens the harvest. I have already said that some Grail legend commentators see in the holy object a reflection of the Horn of Plenty and much ink has been spilled in tracing the stories back to pagan fertility cults. This seemed to me a bit far-fetched, and when I came to look at Psalm 67, I was struck by its beauty and confirmed in my opinion that here we had at least one link to support the theory that the Knights of the Round Table were Templars in disguise. Here it is:

> God be mericful unto us and bless us
> *And let the light of thy countenance shine upon us*
> Selah
> That thy way may be known upon earth,
> Thy saving health among all nations.
> Let all the people praise thee, O God: let all the people praise
> thee.
> O let the nations be glad and sing for joy: for thou shalt judge
> the people righteously, and govern the nations upon earth.
> Selah

Then shall the earth bring forth her increase; and God even our
own God, shall bless us.
God shall bless us; and all the ends of the earth shall fear him.

It does not take much imagination to see how the repeated
cry of "Selah" might be mistaken for "Yallah", the Saracen
war-cry. But why on earth, one is entitled to ask, should the
Templars, whose chief object was the defence of Christianity,
give vent to Saracen warcries during their religious
ceremonies? It doesn't make any sense at all. On the other
hand, the references in this psalm to the light of God's countenance and to earth's increase do reflect passages in the Grail
legends which speak of light emanating from the Grail as well
as the nourishment it offers.

The word "Selah" doesn't occur in Psalm 67 only. On the
contrary, it is found in thirty-three others. There is some
doubt as to its precise meaning, but some people think it is a
musical or liturgical direction, perhaps indicating a pause or
rest. It does certainly seem to occur at points in the psalms
which require emphasis. The nearest parallel might be the cry
of "Alleluia" uttered at revivalist services when the congregation finds a statement of the preacher's particularly appealing.
The word is now generally omitted from versions of the psalms
as sung in church. Since the word occurs in the Old Testament versions of the psalms, and since it is so common, it is
out of the question to believe that the Inquisitors did not know
exactly what it was. Hence the accusation that the Templars
were giving vent to Saracen warcries is particularly odious.

I though it would be interesting to examine all the psalms in
which the word "Selah" occurs in the hope that this might
shed some light on our problem. In the end it did; I found that
these psalms contain five common threads which occur in
them, all of which are more or less appropriate to what we
know of Grail and Templar ceremonies.

Psalms 3, 4, 44, 46, 47, 59, 61, 68, 77, 81, 83, 140 and 143 all
betray a consciousness of enmity from without and stress
God's ability to preserve and shield the faithful.

Psalms 24, 50, 66, 67, 68, 75, 84, 85 and 89 stress the
richness and power of God in nature and his gifts to mankind.

Psalms 32, 52, 76, 82 and 85 reveal a sense of guilt and

stress the forgiveness of sins by God. Their underlying theme
can best be summed up in the word Justice.

Psalms 39, 49, 54, 62, 68, 75, 77 and 88 are concerned with
death, redemption and salvation.

Psalms 48, 50, 76 and 87 are concerned with the holiness of
Zion and of the Temple.

I found another clue to link the Templars with the legends
of the Holy Grail and with the ceremonies attached to the
Mandylion when it was in Constantinople. The brethren were
accused by the Inquisition of prostrating themselves before
their "Idol", a custom not followed in the Roman Church but
common enough in the East. It is called proskenesis, and was
accorded only to the Emperor and to specially holy icons and
relics. The practice continued for many centuries in Russia,
where subjects were required to prostrate themselves before
the Tsar. Ivan the Terrible is said to have thrown people out of
the window if they failed for any reason to accord him this
veneration. To find the Templars engaged in this practice
must surely mean that they perhaps acquired it in Constantinople along with the object.

There are references in the answers given by the brethren to
the Inquisition to an unconsecrated Mass which strongly
resembles the ceremony I described in chapter three where the
priest first performed a form of Mass for the Dead, then
retired to let the congregation partake of a "feast" served from
the Grail. Shadowy though this may appear (written perhaps
with the deliberate intention of preserving a sense of mystery
and awe) it is clear that in some way these are superior to
every-day Masses. There is no need for a priest or consecra-
tion since Christ himself presides *in person* and his Real
Presence is visible for all to see within the Grail. In one of the
versions of the legend, Joseph of Arimathea is said to have
been initiated by Jesus in a special sacrament performed with
the Grail, which is superior to the normal Mass. The food
Joseph consumes sustains him for forty-two years in prison. In
other words, we are not dealing here with a pagan cornucopia,
but with a spiritual meal which brings with it eternal life and
salvation.

If the Templars' "Idol" was the Shroud in its latticework
casket, the Grail, then much becomes clear. It is easy to

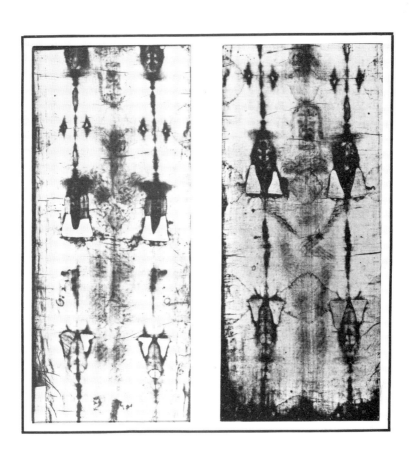

The Holy Shroud
Frontal & Dorsal

understand why the "Vision of God" here displayed was not for the sight of ordinary men. Moreover, this was the privilege not of the Church's clergy, but of the Order's elect. Throughout the Grail legends great emphasis is laid on this aspect of the quest: only those who through the purity of their lives and through their valour have proved themselves worthy are allowed to view the sacred object.

I must close this chapter with an examination of Malory's *Morte d'Arthur*, which although much later is nevertheless firmly based on the earlier versions of the story as they were told in Champagne and Burgundy.

When Galahad is crowned king of Sarras, he keeps the Grail in a temple on a silver table.

> "When the end of the year came round, on the anniversary of the day when he had first won the crown, he and his companions arose early in the morning. And when they came to the temple, they looked at the sacred Vessel, and they saw a handsome man dressed like a bishop and he was on his knees before the table . . . He rose and began the Mass of the Glorious Mother of God. And when he came to the mystery of the Mass and had removed the platter from the sacred Vessel, he called Galahad and said to him: 'Come forward, servant of Jesus Christ, and thou shalt behold what thou hast desired to see.' Then Galahad stepped forward and looked within the sacred Vessel. And when he looked in, he began to tremble violently, as soon as mortal flesh began to gaze on the things of the spirit. Then Galahad stretched forth his hand toward Heaven, and said: 'Lord, I adore thee and thank thee that thou hast brought my desire to pass, for now I see clearly what tongue could not tell nor heart conceive. Here I behold the motive of courage and the inspiration of prowess; here I see the marvel of marvels."

Once more I ask you to picture in your mind's eye the Shroud as we now know it; picture to yourself the photographs which show so vividly the terrible wounds inflicted upon Jesus by the vicious flagrum; picture to yourself the traces of blood on his arms and forehead and the deep scar in his side; read the unemotional medical account of Dr David Willis where he describes the nature of Jesus's wounds and the action upon his hands and feet of the nails that were driven through them; think of the slow death by suffocation; remember that he was beaten over the head and face till the eyes and nose were bruised and swollen, and how, having gone through all this he was forced to carry the heavy, wooden cross-beam from Pilate's Courtroom to Golgotha: no words in any language are adequate to express the anguish he underwent. That this torture was undergone for altruistic motives cannot fail to move the greatest sceptic and the most hardened cynic. How much more must these things have moved men in the age of faith?

There are other significant points to notice in Malory's account. First, the celebration of the Mass of the Glorious Mother of God recalls the strong association we know to have existed between the Mandylion and the Virgin Mary. This was recognised on the coinage issued by the Emperor Constantine Porphyrogenitus when he brought the relic to Byzantium in the year 945; timing its arrival to coincide with the Feast of the Assumption and keeping a copy of the relic in the church of St Mary of Blachernae. It is also a reminder of the claims of Byzantine clerics that the relic was veritable proof of the incarnation of Jesus within Mary. This also supports Geoffrey Ashe's view that at the moment of supreme vision, the Grail, as the vessel of the revelation of God Incarnate was really Mary in symbolic form.

Second, Galahad's trembling recalls the fear some of the Templars said they felt when approaching the "Idol" for the first time. Above all, the sequences in Malory which read "Come forward and behold . . ." and "Lord I adore thee . . ." find an exact echo in the historically reported words of the Templar Visitor General at the secret ceremony in the presence of the "Idol" who said:

"Come, let us go and adore him who has made us and not left us."

All this drove me to conclude that just as the Byzantines regarded Christ as being literally present in the Mandylion, so did the Templars in the presence of their "Idol", and that this was written into the Grail legends. Both the Templars and the Knights of the Round Table believed that Christ "lived among them". The "Super-Mass" ceremony in the Real Presence of Christ in both history and legend was the core of

the secret which the Templars died to defend; the Shroud/
Mandylion/Grail that lay at the heart of it the very holy of
holies of their Order.

## SEVEN

HAVING ESTABLISHED the similarities between Templar ceremonial and that associated with the Grail in most of the legends, let us look at the history of the Order itself to see what light that might throw upon the question of when the Shroud and the Grail came into its possession and when they were brought to France.

In November 1307, some six weeks after the attack on the Order by King Philip the Fair, four senior brethren were interrogated after torture in Paris. One of them was the Grand Master, Jacques de Molay, the others were Hugues de Pairaud, the Visitor of France, to all intents and purposes the "second-in-command", Geoffrey de Charnay, the Master of Normandy and Guy d'Auvergne. Questioned about the "Idol", Hugues de Pairaud had this to say: "He had seen, held and touched it at Montpellier at a Chapter there, and that he and the other brothers had adored it . . . Required to declare the place where it is now he said that he sent it to Pierre Allemandi, Preceptor of the House of Montpellier, but he did not know if the King's men found it. He said the 'head' had four feet, two in front on the side of the face and two behind." (Dixit quod dictum caput habebat quattuor pedes, duos ante ex parte faciei et duos retro.)

Hugues de Pairaud said he had been received into the Order by Brother Humbert de Pairaud, his uncle, forty years before, that is to say about 1267. Pierre Allemandi was Preceptor of Montpellier in 1265 and then from 1267 to 1304.

103

Painting by Giulio Clovio (XVI Century)

Without doubt, this was the most unequivocal evidence I have found that the Mandylion did belong to the Templars, for imagine to yourself what the Shroud looks like when fully unfolded. It is, as I have said, about fourteen feet in length, and when the body was laid on it, the other half was folded over the head and came down to reach the feet. Thus there is a double image of Jesus' body on it, which is joined at the head giving one the impression that the image has four legs, two on the front and two at the back. It would be hard to find a clearer description of the Shroud of Turin than Hugues de Pairaud's. Furthermore, it gives us firm dates between which the relic was in Montpellier. When did it arrive and when did it leave?

The Templars of Montpellier were particularly compromised in the eyes of the Inquisition on account of the presence of the "idol" there. Furthermore, Montpellier was the senior Grand Priory and thus the *de facto* headquarters of the Order after the fall of Acre, at least until 1293. Some of the brethren described it as a "tête de mort" or death's head, which could either indicate a skull or the head of a dead man. This, not unnaturally, gave rise to the false accusation of idolatry. Nothing resembling either the "idol" or the Shroud was found in the Temple Church of Nôtre Dame de Lèze, although all the Order's valuables there were seized by the King's officers.

The evidence of Brother Bernard de Selgues, Knight Commander of the Preceptory of Saint Gilles, and thus a senior member of the Order, is typical of many others. He said he had taken part in provincial chapters (Saint Gilles (Gard) was closely associated with the Grand Priory of Montpellier), and at one of these held at Montpellier, which assembled at night "according to custom" "on y exposa un chef ou une tête". This head (it is impossible to translate *chef* by any other word, but the distinction between that word and *tête* seems to indicate that it was in some way special) had promised the brethren a good harvest, the possession of riches and all manner of good things. He went on to say that he had adored the head along with all the other brethren present.

This evidence seems to reflect closely the words of psalm 67 or one of the other "Selah" psalms I mentioned in the last chapter.

Brother Raoul de Gise confirmed Hugues de Pairaud's evidence, but added that the "idol" had a terrible countenance, and that when they were shown it they all prostrated themselves on the ground and pulled their cowls over their heads. This is another reason why, in a darkened chapel at dead of night, they had little chance of examining it closely, hence their vague descriptions of it.

Brother Raimond de Fabre de Montbazin said he attended about ten General Chapters of the Order at Montpellier, which were usually attended by senior brethren as well as by Commanders of Houses from far and wide. For example, he was at a General Chapter held on May 9 1284 which was attended by the Master of the Order in Provence (Pierre Allemandi) and the Commanders of Le Puy (Haute-Loire), St Gilles (Gard), Saint-Eulalie-de-Larzac (Aveyron), Richerenches (Vaucluse) and Bras(Var). The General Chapter of 1293 was held under the chairmanship of the Grand Master, Jacques de Molay. The last Chapter was held in 1305 by Guige d'Adhémar, Master of Provence.

The Temple buildings at Montpellier were very large. After the Order's dissolution they were given to the Knights of St John of Jerusalem and thenceforth the church became known as Grand-Saint-Jean. During the Order's two centuries of existence Montpellier became increasingly important on account of its geographical position at the crossroads of the routes from Spain to Italy and Germany and from the north of France, the Low Countries and England to the Holy Land. It was customary for those about to embark on a Crusade to lodge there before embarking at Aigues Mortes, and many kings, princes and barons were entertained there. Because it was so near the sea, Montpellier would have been the obvious place to house the Mandylion/Grail when it first arrived in France from Hungary. According to Hugues de Pairaud, this must have been after 1290, since he did not hold office until about that year. We still lack all knowledge of the Shroud's movements between the time it came into the hands of the Templars in Hungary and the reign of Pierre Allemandi as Commander of the House at Montpellier. Consequently, we can only guess that it arrived sometime between 1242 and 1290 and that it was removed before 1304. Whenever it was, we can be certain that the acquisition of such a valuable relic would have had the attention of the Grand Master and senior members of the Order.

From its foundation to its dissolution there were twenty-three Grand Masters altogether. Those in whom we are interested were the following:-

| | |
|---|---|
| Pierre de Montaigu | 1219-1232 |
| Armand de Périgord | 1232-17/20 Oct 1244 |
| Guillaume de Sonnac | 1245-3 July 1250 |
| Renaud de Vichier | 1250-19 Jan 1252 |
| Thomas Beraud | 1252-25 March 1273 |
| Guillaume de Beaujeu | 13 May 1273-18 May 1291 |
| Thibaud Gaudin | August 1291-16 April 1292 |
| Jacques de Molay | End of 1292-11 March 1314 |

Pierre de Montaigu was Master of Aragon and then of Provence before his election as Grand Master in 1218. He had spent the greater part of his earlier career in Spain and was still Master of Provence in 1219. He does not seem to have taken up his post as Grand Master until nearly a year after his election. He was at St Gilles during the earlier part of the Albigensian Crusade, which lasted from 1209 to 1219. Not a great deal is known about him, and nothing that could link him with the Mandylion or with Hungary.

Pierre's immediate successor, Armand de Périgord, was Preceptor of Sicily and Calabria and is known to have spent most of his term of office in Cyprus, so it is unlikely that he played any part in the transaction by which the Templars obtained the Shroud. Next to nothing is known of Renaud de Vichier, beyond the fact that he was a friend of Jean de Joinville. He became Marshal of the Order in about 1246 and took part in the Battle of Mansourah in 1250. His tenure of office lasted no more than two years, and by the time his successor was elected, the Shroud must surely have belonged to the Templars.

The list of Treasurers, who were ex-officio Grand Priors of Champagne, is less complete that the list of Grand Masters. Jean de Milly, who was probably a Burgundian, may have been Treasurer at the vital time, for he is known to have been

in office in 1234. The next Treasurer is known only as Brother
Gilles, and he served from 1234 to 1250, but after him there is
a gap in our knowledge until 1278 when Jean de la Tour was
appointed. He was Commander of Étampes at the time of his
appointment, and he died in 1302.

After the fall of Acre in 1291, which brought to an end the
Frankish kingdoms in the Holy Land, the Order was forced to
move its headquarters. Immediately following this catastrophe, the Grand Master, Thibaud Gaudin, established himself
in Cyprus, but his tenure of office lasted little more than
eighteen months.

Jacques de Molay, another Burgundian, was elected Grand
Master at the end of 1292, at a time when the Order's affairs
were in disarray. His election was the subject of considerable
dissension. A large number of influential brethren supported
Hugues de Pairaud, but not enough to be decisive. Although
de Molay died a martyr's death, his term of office was un-
distinguished, being marked by vacillation and indecision.

In the early autumn of 1307, King Philip the Fair arrived at
the abbey of Maubuisson where he stayed for a fortnight. He
had with him the Archbishop of Narbonne, Gilles Aycelin, the
Keeper of the Great Seal of France, Guillaume de Paris and
Guillaume de Nogaret, his closest adviser. They discussed the
king's plan to suppress the Order, but the archbishop objected
because he considered it illegal. It was, he said, within the
power of the Pope alone to act against the Templars, and he
warned the king that any action he might take could once
more awaken the quarrel between the spiritual and temporal
power. Nogaret and de Paris were more subtle. They said that
the king should proceed against the French Templars as
individuals, but the archbishop would have none of this. In the
end the King over-ruled him, and the order to arrest the
Templars was signed on September 23 1307 at Maubuisson,
and Nogaret hastened to put it into effect. Secret orders were
sent to all the seneschals of France to arrest all the brothers on
October 13 and to seize everything of value in their houses.

Jean de Vergy, Seigneur de Fouvent, de Champlitte, de
Mirebeau, grandfather of Jeanne de Vergy, and Jean de
Joinville, grandfather of her husband, Geoffrey de Charny, the
Porte-Oriflamme, were respectively seneschals of Burgundy

and Champagne. They would, without doubt, have received these orders not later than the end of September or the first week in October. However, between September 23 and October 17, 1307, the Court of Burgundy had other things to think about. During this period there were great festitivities in Dijon connected with the marriage of Duke Robert II's daughter, Blanche, to Edward, son of Count Amadeus of Savoy. This event must, without doubt, have demanded the presence not only of Jean de Vergy, the bride's cousin, (for they were great-nephew and great-niece respectively of the late Duchess Alix de Vergy), but also of Guillaume de Mont-Saint-Jean, one of the bride's uncles. It is less certain if Jean de Charny, Guillaume's cousin would have had to be present. He, of course, was the son-in-law of Jean de Joinville, and subsequent events suggest that it was he who was entrusted with the task of warning the Grand Prior of Champagne of the Order's impending fate. Jacques de Molay does not seem to have received any warning, or if he did, he ignored it.[1] This would have been in keeping with his character. It is true that he had had a conference with the Pope on August 24 to discuss the King's hostility to the Order, but on the very eve of the arrests, October 12, he attended the funeral in Paris of the King's sister-in-law, Catherine de Valois. If the Shroud had been in Paris, and if there had been any plan to save it, de Molay does not appear to have known about it. Obviously, the Grand Master must have known where the Shroud was kept, and his behaviour, for whatever reason, suggests unconcern for its safety.

Jean de Vergy and Jean de Joinville, on the other hand, not only knew the King's plans, they had many reasons for warning the Templars of what was about to happen to them. Though it may have been impolitic as well as impractical to prevent their arrest, they undoubtedly had the motive and opportunity to save the Shroud. In such an emergency, it would not have been difficult to remove the linen cloth from its golden casket, wrap it round the body of a horseman, who could have taken it away under his cloak entirely undetected.

---

[1] His brother was Dean of Langres.

All I had to do now was discover where the Shroud might have gone after its disappearance from Montpellier.

The period following the expulsion of the Order from Palestine in 1291 was, as I have already said, one of great difficulty and readjustment. There must have been a good deal of debate among the brethren before any decision was taken concerning the Shroud. Care for its safety must have been always uppermost in their minds, and they had to choose a house that was both secure and easily accessible from all over Europe. It did not necessarily follow that this should be the same as the headquarters of the Order, for the Shroud's religious role in the life of the Order was different from every other and had nothing to do with its political or financial activities. With the loss of the Holy Land, the Order's centre of gravity had shifted to western Europe. Montpellier was no longer at the crossroads; Italy, Aragon, England, Germany and Castile were too far from the geographical centre of things. The two Houses in Paris were too close to the increasingly hostile King of France, Auvergne, Aquitaine and Normandy were too remote from the rest of Europe. A glance at the map will show that Voulaines was the obvious place to choose, partly because the Order had grown up in Champagne and Burgundy, but also on account of its geographical situation. There seems little doubt that the Shroud must have been sent there, and that it was removed from Voulaines either to the château de Mont-Saint-Jean or to Charny or Vergy before the King attacked.

The first thing that strikes the visitor to Mont-Saint-Jean is the unusually large number of stone crosses, or *"Calvaires"* in the immediate vicinity of the village. I counted no fewer than twenty-five within a radius of less than eight kilometers, and there are five in the village itself. This suggests that the church, or village was once a centre of pilgrimage. In the Middle Ages, Mont-Saint-Jean was an important place with more than fifteen hundred inhabitants. It possessed a hospital, a covered market and great priory church in addition to its castle and parish church. One of the Lords of Mont-Saint-Jean is said to have brought back from the Holy Land the relics of Saint Pelagia, but whether this alone can account for the large number of "calvaires" is arguable. It is impossible to say how long the Shroud may have remained there, or whether these crosses were erected for pilgrims to its shrine or that of St Pelagia. If, as I believe, it came into the possession of the de Charny-Mont-Saint-Jean family in 1307, it is probable that they kept it either in the safety of their domestic chapel within the castle keep or in the parish church within the castle precincts until such time as Geoffrey de Charny built a special church for it on his estates at Lirey in 1356.

It is not, perhaps, without significance to discover that the present Sieur de Mont-Saint-Jean and Seigneur de Charny is none other than the son of the late King of Italy.

# PART FIVE
*The Treasure of Montségur*

# EIGHT

IF THE "IDOL" of the Templars was in reality the Shroud of Christ and the Holy Grail the latticework casket in which it was kept, this still left me wondering whether Wolfram von Eschenbach's Stone Grail might be the Keramion, and if so whether this relic was the mysterious Cathar treasure. Superficially it seemed a hypothesis worth following up, but I had to ask myself how it came into the possession of these heretics and when.

Languedoc, the home of the Cathars has had a rather different history from the rest of France. When the Roman Empire was in decline it became for a while a Jewish principality, but was later conquered by the Visigoths at the time the Franks were making their great inroads in the north. The Visigoths practiced an unorthodox form of Christianity called Arianism, and this tradition of separateness persisted through the centuries, and led eventually to the adherence by a large section of the population to another heresy derived from Manichaeism, which reached here from the Balkans, and ultimately from Persia. The heartland of the heresy was the region of Albi, and the Church's attempt to stamp it out became known as the Albigensian Crusade.

When I began this search I was struck by a series of apparent coincidences which seemed to demand further examination. They were these: Constantinople was sacked in April 1204; at the end of May that year Pope Innocent III set up a commission led by Arnaud Aimary and Pierre de

115

Castelnau and made up of monks from Cîteaux and Font-froide with full authority to do all they could to stamp out Catharism; in 1205 orders were given to the owner of Mont-ségur to refurbish the castle, and within a year or two it became the principal centre of pilgrimage for the Cathars; in 1207 a meeting was held at Pamiers between the Cathars and representatives of the Pope with the ostensible intention of reconciling the two faiths. It broke down in May of that year, and was quickly followed by an order from the Pope to excom-municate Raymond VI, Count of Toulouse. In January 1208, the Papal legate, Pierre de Castlenau was assassinated in Toulouse, thus providing the Pope with a *casus belli*. The Albigensian Crusade was launched the following year, culminating thirty-five years later in the holocaust of Mont-ségur. Stories of the Cathar treasure persist to the present day. The Nazi writer, Otto Rahn had believed that it was the Holy Grail and claimed that Wolfram's *Parzival* was set in the Pyrenees around Montségur. The latest theory claims that the treasure was, indeed, the Holy Grail, but that this was a secret known to the Cathars and consisted in the knowledge of the true descendants of Jesus, in other words the Sang Real or True Bloodline. How does this look in the light of my discovery of the links between the Mandylion and the Keramion on the one hand and the Templars and the Grail legends on the other?

Catharism derives from a heresy known as Bogomilism, which arose in the tenth century in Bulgaria. By the twelfth century it had taken a strong hold in Macedonia, Thrace, Bosnia and Dalmatia. Its centre there was at Trogir which had originally been a Greek settlement and later a Roman town. In the twelfth century it was sacked by the Saracens and its inhabitants were dispersed among the villages on the mainland. That, however, did not prevent the city from embracing Catharism when it reached there from Bosnia. Bogomilism and Catharism derive from Manichaeism, which in its origin was a reaction against the extreme fatalism of Zoroastrianism, which held that man's destiny was decided by the stars. Mani created the myth that showed the universe as a field for moral effort. Inspired by Christianity, he imagined that in the beginning of time there had been a kingdom of light and a kingdom of darkness existing side by side without any contact or mixture, and that these had later been confused as a result of agression on the part of the powers of darkness. This was the origin of the present world, and it became the duty of men who were on the side of light, (which he identified as virtue and reason), to recover the particles of light that had been imprisoned in the substance of darkness, which was identified as vice and wickedness.

By 1167 this heresy had reached the south of France and by then was well established there. A council was held in that year at Saint-Felix-de-Lauragais, not far from Toulouse, under the auspices of the Cathar Patriarch, Nicetas, of Constantinople to establish Cathar bishoprics in the west based on the model of those in Bulgaria, Macedonia and Dalmatia. By the end of the century Catharism had spread so far throughout Languedoc that it almost became the local orthodoxy. This posed a threat to the Catholic Church and the continued independence of the region became an increasing source of irritation to the King of France, who aimed to control more firmly his over-powerful vassals. The ultimate outcome of the Albigensian Crusade was the total suppression of the heresy and the absorption of Languedoc into the kingdom of France.

In spite of certain non-Christian elements in Catharism, such as the belief in reincarnation, for example, the Cathars regarded themselves as Christians. They rejected the usual Christian sacraments, and replaced them instead with a single one, which they called the Consolamentum, a ceremony not unlike baptism. Their preachers were of both sexes and known as Parfaits and Parfaites (Perfects). They laid great emphasis on personal contact with God, the source of all goodness, but the body and all things physical were of the substance of darkness and hence Satanic. As a result they denied the divinity of Jesus, since He must be either all spirit, in which case His appearance on earth was purely illusory, or He must have been a mortal prophet, and hence not the Son of God. This did not mean that the Cathars rejected His sacrifice for mankind on the Cross. On the contrary, they accorded Him the highest veneration in much the same way that Unitarians do today. All this had a profound effect upon their attitude to relics. Since the majority of these were physical and material in character, they rejected them out of hand. The bones of saints and suchlike had no meaning for them; the Keramion, on the other hand, with its miraculous image of Christ not made by human hands might have been another matter altogether. Of all the relics of the Passion, the Shroud and the Keramion alone would have come closest to being acceptable to the Cathars. It seems, therefore, that this notion of the nature of the treasure is the only tenable one. If it were not the Keramion, then it must have been something totally different, such as an ancient codex or other writings of particular value to them.

Montségur is situated on land which belonged to Guy de Lévis, suzerain of Mirepoix, though the castle itself was the property of Esclarmonde, sister of Count Raimond-Roger de Foix. It was held by Raimond de Pérella, her vassal, and it was to him the order was given towards the end of 1204 for the refurbishing of the castle, which had been allowed to fall into a state of disrepair.

The first phase of the Albigensian Crusade lasted from 1209 to 1229. There followed a lull during which Montségur became the Cathar stronghold *par excellence*, which it remained until its capture in 1244. Many believers came there to stay for longer or shorter periods; to climb up to the castle from the village at the foot of the mighty rock upon which it stands; to take part in the religious services there; to venerate the Parfaits and to depart at length to take up once more their outward lives as good Catholics, for it has to be remembered that many Cathars were obliged outwardly to conform to the orthodoxies of their neighbours.

For ten years Montségur was at the very heart of Cathar resistance to Catholic persecution. From Spain dispossessed knights who owned nothing but their arms and their faith crossed the mountains to gather together in this high place where the kind of worship in which they so profoundly believed was carried on with a solemnity which equalled, and even surpassed, that of the period immediately before the war when the Cathars enjoyed greater freedom than they did then.

As the capital of the Cathar church in Languedoc, Mont-

Chateau de Montségur          Copyright Yan ou Jean Dieuzaide

Montségur showing main portal     Reportage Photographique Yan

ségur housed not only a large number of the sect's ministers and officials, insofar as these differed from the Parfaits, but also its treasure. This certainly consisted of silver and gold, since considerable sums of money were needed to defend the castle as well as to maintain its garrison and those who were living in it. It almost certainly comprised something else. This might have included sacred books, ancient manuscripts or the works of venerated masters – it almost certainly did. But was there anything more? Could there have been relics or other sacred objects? It is certain that none of the depositions taken by the Inquisition after Montségur was captured ever mention anything of the kind. At the same time the Inquisitors' interrogatories, which the heretics were compelled to answer under threat of torture, never included anything relating to this subject. In other words there is nothing tangible to go on, yet the legend of the treasure must certainly have some foundation in fact, and was certainly something beyond mere gold and silver.

There are good reasons for being suspicious of what has come to be known as the Cathar theory concerning the Holy Grail. The Templars, whom I hope to have shown were the owners of the Shroud, were orthodox Catholics, and their "idolatry", if it ever existed outside the biassed imagination of their persecutors, differed from the Cathar heresy except in one singular respect. Both were accused by their enemies of worshipping a "Head". I discussed the possible connection between Wolfram's Munsalvaesche and Montségur in the first chapter; it is now time to look at this in more detail to see whether it can be justified or not. Fortunately we have a firm date before which there was no possibility of the Cathar treasure being one of the relics of Christ's Passion, for until April 1204 the Mandylion and the Keramion were safely housed in Constantinople. Since Cathar theology was unlikely to have permitted the veneration of any other kind of relic, it has to be shown that the legend relating to the Cathar treasure post-dates 1204. If the theory that Wolfram wrote *Parzival* with Montségur and the Ariège in mind, then I must demonstrate that he did so after that date too.

Professor Hatto, the translator of *Parzival* advances good reasons for believing the poem was written between 1205 and

1208. Part of his theory hinges on when Wolfram incorporated Lohengrin into it. Lohengrin, for those who do not know the story, was Parsifal's son and Duke of Brabant, so Wolfram says, by marriage. The historical Duke Henry I of Brabant was on Crusade in 1197; between then and 1203 he had no son. In 1198 his daughter, Marie, was betrothed to Otto of Poitou, but the marriage did not take place immediately. In 1204 the Pope authorised Duke Henry to name Marie his heiress, as it did not then seem as though he would have a son of his own. However, a son *was* eventually born in 1207, but the permission to make Marie the heiress was not revoked, and she finally married Otto in 1214. Consequently until at least 1207 the inheritance of Brabant was through the female line, so Hatto concludes that the inclusion of Lohengrin as Duke of Brabant by marriage must date this part of the poem to before Duke Henry's son was born. Hence the date of the poem as a whole falls between 1205 and 1207. It is true that Wolfram revised parts of the poem later, but commentators are in general agreement that the bulk of it was written *after* the sack of Constantinople. Consequently there is no literary objection to this hypothesis.

Otto Rahn's theory to a great extent depends on whether one can accept that the *Lapis Exilis* was indeed the Keramion, for Cathar theology would not have accepted the Stone of Unction as worthy of veneration, supposing that this was what Wolfram had in mind. As a material object, it held no meaning at all for them. Rahn, of course, never associated the Shroud of Turin with the Grail in any of its forms, because its history was not so well known in his day. Writing in 1934 with the Nazi racial philosophy in the forefront of his mind, one must regard his work with great caution. Nevertheless, the case he advances for believing that Wolfram's source, Kyot der Provenzal, was Guiot de Provins commands rather more respect. Rahn believed that Guiot wrote a version of the Parsifal legend which was lost during the Albigensian Crusades; that is between 1209 and 1244. The first eight chapters of Wolfram's poem are firmly based on Chrétien's *Conte del Graal*, but from chapter nine Rahn maintains that Wolfram gives a completely new interpretation based on Guiot. Whether or not Guiot ever wrote a Grail romance is something we are unlikely now to discover. The fact remains that by the end of the Albigensian Crusade a vast amount of Occitan and Provençal literature was destroyed, chiefly because a substantial number of troubadours were Cathars. All books suspected of heresy were burnt, and only those acceptable to the Catholic Church were saved. This is one reason why it is so hard to arrive at a balanced view of the Cathars and their heresy. Rahn hints that Guiot may have been a Cathar, or at least sympathetic towards them.

Guiot's birthplace, Provins, is a town in Champagne, which was the heartland of the Grail romances. It was also a centre for Catharism as early as the year 1000. From that time onward, Champagne was regarded as the point of departure for Cathar propaganda in northern Europe emanating from its centre at Mont-Aimé, a small town between Troyes and Rheims. The heresy was equally widespread in Burgundy. In 1198, Hugues de Noyers, Bishop of Auxerre asked the Archbishop of Sens for help against the heretics in his diocese, and a conference was held at Charité-sur-Loire the same year to take steps against them. There is no doubt that the heretics in question were Cathars.

Walter Map confirms this in his *De Nugis Curialium*. He, you will recall, wrote this gossipy work between 1182 and 1192, and in it he says there were no Cathars in Normandy or Brittany; he had heard of sixteen only in England, but that in Languedoc and Provence they thrived.

Although a native of Champagne, Guiot talks of Alfonso II of Aragon, who reigned from 1162 to 1196 as his patron and praises his poetic ability and knightly virtue. (Wolfram says in his poem that Kyot derived his information about the Grail legend from a man named Flegetanis in Spain). Alfonso was the rival of Arnaut de Mareuil for the favours of Adelaide de Burlat, daughter of Count Raymond V of Toulouse, and wife of Roger Taillefer de Trencavel, Viscount of Carcassonne. Raymond V, you will remember, allied himself to Richard Coeur de Lion against the King of France, following Richard's return from captivity, and his son, the future Raymond VI, Adelaide's brother, married Richard's sister, Jeanne Plantagenet. The wedding festivities, it will be remembered were known as the Fête de Beaucaire. It is not known whether

Guiot was there but it is a fact that he travelled extensively throughout France and Spain. It is almost certain that he visited Toulouse and Aragon, and to get to the Court of King Alfonso he would have had to take one of two routes. He could either go up the valley of the Ariège by way of Foix, the residence of Raymond-Roger, Count of Foix (a cousin of Roger Trencavel, Viscount of Carcassonne) pass through the region known as the Sabarthés and cross the Col de Puymorens into Spain. At Foix he would have met Esclarmonde, a celebrated beauty, later to become a parfaite, and then the owner of Montségur. On the other hand, he might have gone to Spain by way of Carcassonne and Perpignan. He would have met Esclarmonde's aunt, Adelaide, at Carcassonne, a city she had ruled since her husband's death in 1193 with the love and affection of her subjects. Thus, Guiot must have been familiar not only with the leading nobility of the region, but also with its geography.

If, indeed, Wolfram did base his poem on a lost work of Guiot's, its date of composition is once more of vital importance. Rahn agrees with Hatto that the poem must have been written between 1200 and 1210, but he is no more precise than that. At the same time it can be safely assumed that he was aquainted with the Cathars and their beliefs, even if he did not happen to share them, just as Walter Map was. Rahn makes out that much of what Wolfram wrote into *Parzival* reflects Cathar philosphy and ritual. On closer examination, however, I was unable to accept his reasons as I shall tell in a moment.

So, if Wolfram is to be believed, someone must have read both Guiot's and Chrétien's poems to him, unless he met both poets and heard them recite them themselves. There is a possibility that he might have met one or both of them at the gathering of troubadours in Mainz or a few years later at the Court of the Landgrave Hermann of Thuringia, the Wartburg, in 1203. Wolfram's rudimentary knowledge of French may, thinks Rahn, account for some of the curious names he uses in the poem. Alfonso II of Aragon, for instance, was known in France as Alphonse le Chaste, whom Rahn identifies with Castis, King of Waleis and Norgals. Herzeloyde, Parsifal's mother, he suggests, was none other than Adelaide of Carcassonne, the "domina" or "Fair Lady"

to whom King Alfonso paid court. Adelaide's son was a
member of the Trencavel family, which Rahn tried to make
out means "One who cuts well". Wolfram translates the name
"Parzival" as "Schneid mitten durch", which in English
means "Cuts through the middle". It strikes me that both
Rahn's and Wolfram's etymology is somewhat far-fetched,
but Rahn does not confine himself to the names of people. He
equates Beaucaire with Wolfram's Castle of Bearosche and
the Bois des Priscilliens which lies near Montségur in the
Sabarthés, as the Forest of Briziljan. In a word, Rahn maintains that Wolfram's characters and places can all be
identified through Guiot's lost work with members of the
ruling houses of Anjou, Aragon, Foix, Toulouse, Carcassonne,
Comminges and Plantagenet, and the places in which they
lived in France, Spain and Flanders. In particular he identifies
the female guardian of the Grail, whom Wolfram calls
Repanse de Schoye with Esclarmonde de Foix.

When Rahn comes to identify traces of Catharism in
Wolfram's poem he gets somewhat carried away. Trevrizent,
Parsifal's hermit uncle, he says, *must* be a Cathar because he is
a vegetarian. It is true that the pious Cathars were
vegetarians, but in the Middle Ages, all vegetarians were
regarded with suspicion by the Church. Indeed, one of the
ways you could tell a heretic, it was thought, was by his pale,
anaemic complexion. But then the seventeenth century
Puritans were also accused of looking sickly and pale, and no
one has ever accused them of being vegetarians. This is what
Wolfram has to say about Trevrizent:

> "He had forsworn wine, mulberry and bread. His austerity
> imposed further abstinence: he had no mind for such food as fish
> or meat or anything with blood. Such was the holy life he led . . .
> He endured much hardship from fasting. Self-denial was his
> arm against the devil."

I have to admit that Trevrizent's wish to abstain from meat in
order to conquer the power of the devil is not inconsistent with
Cathar belief, but then there were countless orthodox hermits
and ascetics who followed an equally rigorous diet and
mortified their flesh to attain salvation.

In the poem, Trevrizent lived in a cell near the Fontaine la

Salvaesche beneath an overhanging rock with a waterfall gushing through it. The cell was made from a grotto in the mountainside in which there was an altar-stone on which stood a reliquary. On the slenderest evidence Rahn identifies this with the Grotte de l'Ermite near the great caves of Lombrives in the Ariège valley not far from Ornolac and Tarascon-sur-Ariège. From this and much more, Rahn infers that Wolfram was well acquainted with the geography of the Sabarthés and claims that his description of the country round Munsalvaesche closely tallies with that round Montségur.

To sum up: there seems some evidence to support the view that Wolfram's Kyot was in reality Guiot de Provins; there are less solid grounds for believing that either Guiot or Wolfram had the Cathars in mind, but enough to make further investigation worth the effort. Let us turn again to historical events and see how they fit these theories.

The years 1204 to 1209 seem to be critical to our study. With the failure of the Conference at Pamiers in 1207, the danger threatening the Cathars became much more apparent. The year before, Gaucelm, the Cathar Patriarch of Aquitaine had called a meeting of several hundred parfaits and parfaites at the castle of Pierre-Roger de Mirepoix, subsequently the commander of the Montségur garrison. Gaucelm made it clear that the Roman Church, faced with the impossibility of crushing the heresy by means of missions and conferences, would ultimate resort to force. It was at this conference, according to Rahn, that it was decided to ask Esclarmonde and her vassal, Raymond de Pérella, to take steps to refurbish Montségur as a last refuge in case the papal and royal forces attacked them. This may, indeed, have been one reason, but it does not account for the conversion of Montségur into a place of pilgrimage.

When the Cathars were free to worship as and where they would, Montségur was *not* a holy place – except for those who lived in the region of Foix, the local spirit of independence operating there as anywhere else. All the same, its situation and reconstruction show that it was fitted up with a view to religious worship at a time when the Cathars felt themselves strong enough to build and consecrate their own sactuaries just as the Catholics did. Thus between 1206 and 1243 the

castle became increasingly a holy place of special importance.
People came there *in extremis*, often to die in the shadow of its
walls; pilgrims flocked there by the hundred. This is not likely
to have happened unless there were special religious reasons
for doing so.

Esclarmonde received the Consolamentum some time in
1206, and from that time forth began to play a leading part in
the religious life of Montségur. At this point it is appropriate
to point out that one of the accusations levelled against the
Cathars as well as against the Templars was that of
homosexual practices. In the case of the Cathars this arose
from the custom of parfaits and parfaites working together in
pairs of the same sex in permanent bonds of brotherhood and
sisterhood. I was struck, when I discovered this, by the
frequent references in the Grail legends to pairs of youths and
maidens in attendance on the holy vessel at ceremonies in
which it appeared.

These events suggested to me that perhaps they occurred as
a result of the arrival at Montségur of the Keramion, following
the sack of Constantinople. If such a unique relic did arrive at
this time, this would account both for the refurbishing of
Montségur and its rapidly increasing popularity as a place of
pilgrimage. Assuming for the moment that this was the case, it
would also explain the intensified efforts of the Papacy to
stamp out the heresy, in the process of which the relic might
be returned to orthodox custody. For this to have happened it
is necessary to explain how it might have fallen into the hands
of the Cathars in the first place. There seem to be two
possibilities, neither of them, I have to admit, totally convincing. But before I consider these, let me continue with the
history of these eventful years.

There is no doubt that the Cathar hierarchy, so far as there
was one, made Montségur its headquarters. Guilharbert de
Castres, Raimond Aiguilher and Bertrand Marty, who
between them held the senior offices in the Cathar diocese of
Toulouse and Razès from about 1220, received at Montségur
a large number of knights who played leading roles in the
struggle for independence. Guilharbert, who was by then well
on in years, made numerous trips to castles in the region, all of

them in great secrecy, perhaps to prepare alternative hiding places for the treasures of Montségur.

Possibly the strangest aspect of the castle is its architecture. It was not the only residence of Raimond de Pérella, Seigneur de Montségur, but the building had existed before the establishment of that family in the district, and its construction seems to go back to no earlier than the ninth century. Montségur is one of those rare ruins situated in a position which dominates nothing and on a road that leads nowhere. Most medieval castles are built at strategic points to guard cities and roads. There are, of course, churches built on impossible sites associated with miracles or just because they are particularly beautiful: Rocamadour, Mont-Saint-Michel and St Michel de l'Aiguilhe at Le Puy are three that spring to mind. There is, however, no trace of any pagan cult at Montségur, which might justify the building of a temple in such an inaccessible place. Moreover, its architecture does not resemble that of a religious building, and at the same time it is unlike any other fortified, medieval castle either. The strangest features of its construction are its two doors and what remains of the dungeon windows. The latter are wide and lofty, and they lit the upper storey above a vaulted lower room. They would have let in a great deal of light and are in total contrast to the narrow slits which illuminate the lower floor.

No other medieval castle possesses such a monumental doorway as Montségur. It is almost two metres wide and totally unprotected by outworks of any kind. Such portals were a luxury reserved for churches, and as this door was made in the wall when the castle was refurbished in 1205; a detail of this kind shows that the castle was looked upon as something other than a place of defence. The very idea of having a door made in this way has something strange about it and is altogether contrary to the rules of medieval military architecture.

All this gives one to think that Montségur was indeed, either when first built, or later, destined for the practice of worship. Some authorities have suggested that this was a form of sun worship, but none of them have been able to say who the powerful person or people were who could have built such a monumental structure between the ninth and twelfth centuries to practice a religion about which no one had ever found the least trace in that region. If, however, the refurbishing of Montségur was partly undertaken to house some valuable relic extracted from the treasuries of Constantinople, much of this becomes easier to explain.

The siege of the castle began on May 13 1243 and lasted until March 1244. On March 1 the defenders asked for and obtained a two-week truce which expired on March 16. Among the parfaits shut up in the fortress at the time of the capitulation, three at least escaped the stake. During the night of March 16, Pierre-Roger de Mirepoix, the garrison commander, organised the escape by means of ropes suspended over the western face of the cliff upon which the castle is built, of Amiel Aicart and his companion, Hugo, and Poitevin and of a fourth man, whose name is unknown but who may have been a mountain guide or perhaps Poitevin's companion. They were ordered to hide what remained of the treasure and to take it to the hiding place in which the Parfaits Matheus and Pierre Bonnet had taken a substantial quantity of gold, silver and money two months before. On the basis of evidence later given to the Inquisition, this treasure was hidden in the mountain forests of Sabarthés, pending such time as a more secure hiding place could be found.

Pierre-Roger and his knights were the last to leave the castle after the parfaits, women and children. They became, therefore, for a brief period masters of the place once more. It seems that the escape of these four men was fully successful, since neither they nor the treasure they carried was ever found by the Catholic authorities. Apart from these men, no other parfaits could, or perhaps wished to escape the stake. When the truce expired the seneschal and his knights accompanied by the ecclesiastical authorities presented themselves at the main door of the castle. Raymond de Pérella fulfilled his side of the bargain and handed over some two hundred heretics, including himself, to be taken down to be burnt *en masse*.

If Amiel Aicart and his companions were indeed carrying something it was clearly neither heavy nor bulky. If the purpose of arranging for these men to escape was only to pass on the location of the buried treasure, one is entitled to ask why it was necessary to send four men when two would have been enough. It must have been something of great importance to the defenders, for it is inconceivable to me, having seen the west face of the mountain, which is almost as steep as the notorious north face of the Eiger in Switzerland, that anyone should try to descend it at night without an overwhelming reason. The Keramion was neither heavy nor bulky, but neither would books or papers have been.

If the Cathar treasure was the Keramion we must establish how it got to Montségur. It could have been stolen from the Blachernae by a Crusader who was also a Cathar, of which it is known there were a number; on the other hand, it might have been among the relics that Mary-Margaret took with her to Hungary. Strange to relate there seems to be evidence for both of these possibilities.

In chapter five I told how the Tatars invaded Hungary in 1241 driving King Bela and his family to take refuge in Dalmatia. They moved in panic between Split and the fortress of Klis, just behind in the mountains. The shattered army of nobles, soldiers and priests brought with them the head of Saint Stephen and many holy objects from their churches. The king considered Split too unsafe, and taking his queen and their children, ordered the remnant of his forces to follow him to Trogir, which is within a short distance of many islands. Worn out by fatigue, by hunger and fear, they threw themselves down wherever they could. The Tatars came down the coast. Nothing could stop them. They thought the King would be at Split or Klis and they were repulsed at both. But they found their way to Trogir which was built on a small island separated from the mainland by a narrow stretch of water, spanned by a bridge. This the defenders destroyed, and the Tatars were preparing to rebuild it or ford the channel when they received news that their supreme chief, Ogodai, the son of Genghis Khan had died in Asia and that the succession was in dispute. Trogir and Europe breathed again as the hordes withdrew.

Following the establishment of the Latin Empire in Constantinople in 1204, the kingdom of Bulgaria supported the policies of Pope Innocent III. This alliance with Rome proved to be of short duration for the Kings of Bulgaria soon afterwards entered into alliance with the deposed Greek Emperors of Nicea against the Latins. Thirty-three years later, Pope Gregory IX, on the pretext of stamping out heresy, persuaded Bela IV to launch an attack on King John Arsen II of Bulgaria, whom he accused of sheltering heretics in his territory.

There is thus ample evidence to show that the Cathar-Bogomil heresy was as well established in the Balkans as it was in Languedoc and that Trogir was one of its greatest centres. Between 1219 and 1222 the impetus of the first Albigensian Crusade was lost, and the Cathar church in Languedoc, in spite of the serious mauling it had undergone, began to re-assert itself. By 1225 it was strong enough to feel able to hold a council at Pieusse near Limoux, about twenty-four km south of Carcassonne, to consider matters relating to the administration and hierarchy of the church as though it were officially recognised. Two years earlier the Papal Legate, Bishop Conrad de Porto, had summoned his own council of French prelates at Sens, and told them that the Cathars of Bulgaria, Croatia, Dalmatia and Hungary had just elected a new "Pope" and that he had sent an emissary, Barthélemy Cartès to Languedoc to ordain bishops and preach to the people. "We have seen," wrote Bishop Conrad, "this Satan has sent to the diocese of Agen a man of heretical belief named Barthélemy to be their vicar. . . The bishop of the heretics, Vigouroux de la Bacone, shows a baleful respect to him, and has surrendered his see in his favour and transferred himself to the Toulousain. This Barthélemy in his letters, which he has circulated far and wide, describes himself as 'Barthélemy, Servant of the Servants of the Hospital of the Holy Faith, Greetings . . . ' He makes bishops and claims to consecrate churches."[1]

Vigouroux was active in southwest France from 1223 to 1232 and is known to have made journeys to Lauragais, the valley of the Ariège and perhaps to Montségur. Barthélemy's journey to the Balkans, however, cannot be precisely dated.

---

[1] It should be noted that the Roman pontiffs described themselves as the 'Servant of the Servants of Christ'.

Nevertheless it is another coincidence to find this influential Cathar in that part of the world at precisely the time when King Andrew II was so short of money, so there is at least the possibility of the Keramion passing from the ownership of the Hungarian royal family to the Cathars of Languedoc.

Finally, it is perhaps worth mentioning that during the ten years preceding the fall of Montségur, namely from 1234 to 1244, the struggle in Languedoc took on a radically different character. From being primarily a religious conflict it became a struggle for national survival. The earlier Albigensian Crusade had been so horrendous that Cathar and Catholic alike became aware of their common national identity. Their whole way of life and independence was threatened by the agressive centralism of the king. Twenty-five years after the fall of Montségur Philip the Fair finally absorbed Languedoc into his kingdom. If the Keramion did come into the hands of the Cathars, they no doubt looked upon it as a protective talisman in much the same way that the Byzantines had looked upon the Mandylion. As such they would have afforded it the strongest possible protection, and there was nowhere stronger than Montségur. Perhaps we shall never know the truth, for I feel that the evidence for believing that Montségur housed the Grail is very slight. Rahn was not a professional scholar, and his work is full of wild conclusions and unjustified deductions. At the same time it has to be said that he did do some valuable work, and it would be foolish to discount all of it out of hand.

# PART SIX
*The Evidence Reviewed*

# NINE

I HAVE TRIED to take an impartial stand between those who believe the Grail came into the possession of the Cathars and those who think it belonged to the Templars. It is now time to sum up the evidence on both sides.

The image-bearing cloth, known as the Mandylion, probably identical with the Shroud of Turin, was encased in a casket with a golden, latticework cover. One of the origins of the word "Grail" derives from the Old French "Greil" or "Greille", which in turn comes from the Low Latin "Graticula" or "Gradella" and ultimately from the Classical Latin "Cratis", all of which mean lattice, grill or trellis. The other origin of the word derives from the Low Latin "Gradalis" or "Gradalus" and ultimately via the Classical Latin "Cratus" from the Greek " $\kappa\rho\alpha\tau\eta\rho$ " meaning chalice, goblet or cup.

The Mandylion/Shroud was in Constantinople from the middle of the tenth century until April 1204, after which it vanished along with many other relics of the Passion after the city was sacked by the Crusaders. It was housed in the Pharos Treasury with the Keramion, a tile bearing the likeness of Christ 'not-made-by-human-hands' (Akheiropoeitos), the Holy Lance, Nails from the Crucifixion and parts of the True Cross.

Both the Mandylion and the Keramion are known to have played a part in special Masses in Byzantium which appear to resemble ceremonies described in the Grail romances. By

means of some kind of gadgetry the Shroud was exposed in stages to symbolise events of Jesus' earthly life and Passion. The earliest descriptions of the Holy Grail show that
a) it had to do with Christ's Passion
b) it was a vessel containing His blood
c) it had to do with some kind of magical stone
d) it was a series of changing images
e) it was brought to Britain by Joseph of Arimathea
f) it was housed in a castle variously called Corbenic and Munsalvaesche.
The Grail romances began to appear during the last quarter of the twelfth century. The 'Matière de Bretagne' which formed the theme of so much medieval literature of this and the succeeding century was derived, at least in part, from Celtic myths preserved in Ireland, Wales and Cornwall. With the accession of the Plantagenets, French poets and minstrels came to know these works from Britain. Through them they also became well known in Hungary. Henry II found it politic to foster past tales of British glory to rival the splendour which stories about the exploits of Charlemagne shed on the French kings.

The Arthurian legends became popular in the Latin version of Geoffrey of Monmouth written about 1130. It was around this time that Ordericus Vitalis, the British monk, made the west aware of the existence of the Mandylion in Byzantium. Geoffrey of Monmouth's work was translated from Latin into French by the Norman poet, Wace, in about 1155; within the next thirty years, the Grail element was introduced into those stories which had to do with King Arthur and his knights. This development coincided with the foundation and rise to power of the Order of Knights Templar, and both the Order and the romances had their origins in Champagne and Burgundy.

The century following the appearance of Geoffrey of Monmouth's account of the kings of Britain was at first dominated in England (and to a lesser extent in France) by the rivalry between King Stephen and Queen Matilda for the English throne. This was followed by the establishment of the Angevin Empire resulting from the marriage of Henry Plantagenet to

Eleanor of Aquitaine. The last years of Henry II's reign were dominated once more by the question of succession. Following the death of Henry II's son, Geoffrey Plantagenet in 1186, the inheritance devolved upon his posthumous son, Prince Arthur of Brittany. From the moment of his birth, this child became the focus of intrigue between the two contenders for power, Philippe Augustus of France and John Lackland of England, Arthur's uncle. This struggle was intensified following the sudden death of Richard Coeur de Lion in 1199 without direct heirs of his own. Whoever controlled Prince Arthur controlled the Angevin Empire. It comes as no surprise that tales of the legendary King Arthur should have been so popular at this time.

The welding together of the old Celtic, pagan elements with the new Christian ones led to certain internal contradictions and obscurities. But a political thread does run through the romances, for the authors not only set out to entertain their readers but also to promote certain individuals, especially Prince Arthur of Brittany under the disguise of Perceval, the son of the Widow of Anjou. They also included an esoteric element capable of being understood only by a small number of people. A more modern analogy would be Mozart's "Magic Flute", the plot of which is almost incomprehensible to most people, but was quite the reverse to his contempoary Freemasons. Many of the names and terms, especially those to do with the Passion, found in the romances have more than one meaning. The word "Grail" is the most obvious. To some it signified the golden, latticework casket which enshrined the Shroud of Christ; to those who knew nothing of this relic, it signified the Chalice of the Last Supper; to others, like Wolfram, it signified the thin stone or tile, known as the Keramion with its mysterious head of Christ not made by human hand (Akheiropoeitos). All these relics were so holy that only the most pure were allowed to see them; as for the rest of mankind, they had to accept the stories as mysterious without fully understanding their inner meaning.

Between 1175, when the Holy Grail first appears in the Arthurian romances, and 1453 when the Shroud was sold to the Duke of Savoy, the following men and women had some association with both the object and the legends about it. The connection of some was fairly tenuous, but throughout this period of nearly two centuries, one can detect a thread which seems to connect them, quite apart from the thread of kinship.

*Henri de Blois* (ca 1100-1171), brother of King Stephen, Bishop of Winchester, Abbot of Glastonbury.[1]

His nephew: *Henri I, Count of Champagne* (1127-1181). Patron of Chrétien de Troyes, author of earliest Grail romances.

His cousin by marriage: *Pierre de Courtenay*, Latin Emperor of Constantinople (reigned 1216-1219). Father-in-law of *Andrew II of Hungary* (reigned 1205-1235), brother of *Empress Mary-Margaret*, widow of Emperor Isaac Angelus, wife of Boniface de Montferrat. (Also known as Marie de Montferrat.)

His brother: *Robert de Courtenay* (fl 1210). Took part in the Albigensian Crusade.

Their kinsman: *Guillaume de Joinville*, Archbishop of Rheims (1219-1226). Attempted to settle the Albigensian Crusade between the Count of Toulouse and Amaury de Montfort. Patron of Templars of Voulaines.

His brother: *André de Joinville*. Templar – Preceptor of Payns.

Their nephew: *Jean de Joinville* (ca 1228-1318), Seneschal of Champagne, Biographer of Saint Louis.

His daughter: *Marguerite de Joinville* (ca 1250-post 1320), wife of *Jean de Charny*, whose

Second cousin: *Marguerite de Noyers* (fl 1290) was the wife of *Jean de Vergy* (d. 1310) Seneschal of Burgundy.

Their grand-daughter: *Jeanne de Vergy* (pre 1336-post 1389), wife of *Geoffrey de Charny* (ca 1300-1356), her third-cousin-once removed: Porte-Oriflamme de France; first publicly recognised owner of the Shroud.

Their son: *Geoffrey de Charny II* (ca 1355-1398) was praised by his wife's uncle, *Henri de Poitiers*, Bishop of Troyes (fl 1340-1354) for founding the Shroud church at Lirey.

His daughter: *Marguerite de Charny* sold the Shroud to Louis, Duke of Savoy in 1453.

---

[1] King Arthur's grave was said to have been discovered in Glastonbury Abbey 20 years after Bishop Henri's death. Henri was responsible for commissioning the frescoes in the Sepulchre Chapel in Winchester Cathedral, which show Christ in the Shroud.

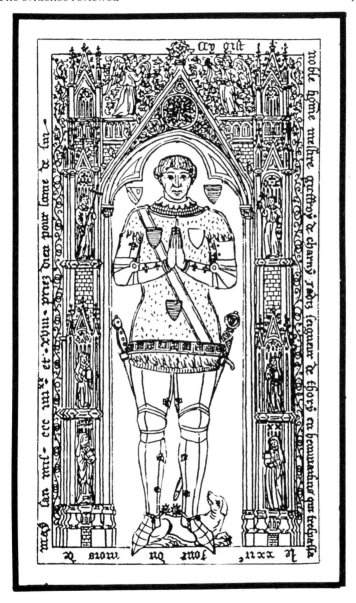

Geoffrey II de Charny. From his tombstone in the abbey of
Froidmont, near Beauvais, France (now destroyed) Bibliothèque
Nationale, Paris.

None of the above appear to have had any family link with Cathar families in Languedoc.

But this does little to solve the problem completely. Why, one may ask, was the Shroud not shown publicly until the middle of the fourteenth century? Assuming that it came into the possession of the Templars in the middle of the thirteenth, I have shown in Part Four why they feared to do so, quite apart from the natural secrecy with which they surrounded so many of their doings. There is, however, a third reason: it was generally believed at the time that the Shroud was in Périgord or Besançon. In 1117, just before the foundation of the Order of Knights Templar, the Cistercian monks of Cadouin had obtained a linen cloth from Antioch, which they and everyone else believed to have been wrapped round Jesus' head at his burial. This "shroud" quickly became the object of a fervent cult, and pilgrims came from all over Europe to see it. Cadouin became rich and famous, and was visited by Richard Coeur de Lion, Saint Louis and King Charles V, to name but three of the better-known pilgrims. I shall consider the Besançon Shroud later.

During the Hundred Years War it was removed to Toulouse for safety, but when the war was over the monks of Cadouin brought it back, but only after lengthy lawsuits and following the intervention of the Pope and King Louis XI. In 1933 this "shroud" was subjected to careful analysis, which proved that it was woven in Egypt in the tenth century.

The question remains: what happened to the Grail? Assuming that the decision to remove the Shroud and its golden latticework casket from Voulaines was taken in a hurry and in great secrecy, it would have been prudent to remove the one from the other. The stone casket of the duc de Blacas, although a blatant forgery, seems to suggest that as late as the end of the eighteenth century there were local traditions round Voulaines of the existence of a relic and of a casket. The duke believed it had held the "idol".

One thing, however, is certain: the casket in which the Shroud was kept when it was in Chambéry was not the lattice-work casket which enclosed the Mandylion. From 1307, therefore, the history of the Shroud separates from that of the Grail.

The Mandylion, and perhaps the Keramion and other relics which vanished after the sack of Constantinople, was taken in all likelihood by Boniface of Montferrat and his wife, the former Empress, to Salonica and lodged in the Basilica of Theotokos. This church is known to have been patronised by "Marie de Montferrat", and was given the name of Hagia Paraskevi (Good Friday) and Akheiropoeitos (Not-made-by-human-hand). As Boniface died in 1207 and the ex-Empress married Nicholas de Saint-Omer the same year, these events must have taken place between 1205 and 1207. The survival of the Keramion is much more doubtful. Because these two relics were kept together in Byzantium is no reason for believing they remained together subsequently. All the other relics were scattered far and wide, and their later history is in many cases well known.

Within a year of the sack of Constantinople, the Cathar hierarchy requested the owner of Montségur to refurbish the castle. If the timing of this request is not purely coincidental, it is not unreasonable to suppose that it might have been in order to house a particularly valuable relic. The Cathars were under no threat of persecution at that time, and had no reason to fear any attack from their local rulers. The architectural peculiarities of Montségur strongly suggest a religious rather than a purely military function. Certainly the religious impor-tance of the place dates from about the time any relic taken from Constantinople would have reached it.

The Cathar religion condemned all material things as the work of the Devil. They denied the physical death of Jesus if He were truly the Son of God for they believed His incarnation was apparent rather than real. If He were wholly human, then He could not have been the Son of God, because God was all goodness and spirit and the flesh was all evil and the creation of Satan. Consequently they rejected the symbolism of the Cross and all the sacraments of the Catholic Church. It is contrary to all logic, therefore, to attribute to the Cathars the veneration of any object so intimately connected with the institution of the Eucharist as the Grail in its Chalice form. No material object of this kind would have had any spiritual meaning for them.

On the other hand, the Mandylion and the Keramion were

different from every other relic because both bore the likeness of Christ "not made by human hands". These relics must have been just as mystifying to those who saw them in the thirteenth century as the Shroud of Turin is to us today. Modern science has not yet been able to offer a convincing naturalistic explanation of how the image got on to the cloth. The best the scientists can say is that it seems to have been the result of heat or light, which explains nothing. The Cathars might therefore have been able to accept one of these relics as worthy of veneration because there was no natural, material explanation for it. Relics like the Crown of Thorns, the True Cross and the rest would have been rejected because of their obvious material nature. In the same way they would have rejected a painting. I have shown that the Cathar relic cannot have been the Shroud; if it were not the Keramion, then it might have been some particularly venerable copy of one of the Gospels – St John's for example, or as Zoe Oldenbourg suggests, ancient documents of special sanctity to the Cathars, but otherwise unknown to us.

Too much stress can be laid on the apparent resemblances between the religious ceremonies of the Templars and what is known of those of the Cathars. Apart from the fact that both were accused of worshipping a bearded head, there is little similarity between them. Nevertheless, the folded Shroud and the Keramion are representations of the bearded head of Christ. This, and the fact that Wolfram's Grail was a thin stone, is all one can say in favour of the Cathar theory as put forward by Otto Rahn and those who have followed in his footsteps. There is no evidence that Wagner ever visited Montségur or that he thought of it as Munsalvaesche. The closest he got was to Monsarrat in Spain.

Although the attitude of the Counts of Toulouse and of the local nobility towards the Cathars was, to say the least, ambivalent where it was not completely tolerant, I can find no evidence of Cathar nobles being members of the Order of Knights Templar. In any society where two religions co-exist as in seventeenth century England, for example, it is possible to find members of both faiths in any given family. Thus there were members of Languedocien families who were Cathars as well as Templars, and so there is nothing inherently unlikely in the idea that members of both may have had a hand in the disappearance of some of the relics from Constantinople. Our problem is to discover what went where, when and to whom.

I can find no firm evidence to identify the Templar Grand Master, Bertrand de Blanquefort with the Cathar nobleman Bertrand de Blanchefort. If, however, the behaviour of Guillaume de Joinville, Archbishop of Rheims and of Pope Clement V in regard to the Cathars seems somewhat equivocal, this does not mean it was on account of the presence of the Grail at Montségur, but rather that these prelates were trying to protect their kinsmen at a time of danger. The most one can say is that there are some fairly slender reasons for believing that the Cathar Grail might have been the Keramion.

The evidence for the Shroud's being in Montpellier at the end of the thirteenth century is much firmer. Hungarian evidence strongly suggests that the Mandylion was removed from Salonica in 1222 and later used by King Bela IV to raise money to reconstruct his country after the Tatars had attacked it in 1241. The presence at Gradac of an early fresco of the head of Christ which closely resembles that on the Shroud; the undoubtedly Slavonic origin of the Laon icon, which states unequivocally that it is the Lord's picture on the cloth; and William de Saint-Omer's epitaph at Trogir, with its bequest of a holy cloth, all seem to point to the same conclusion. None of these snippets of evidence by themselves amount to proof, but taken together with what we know of the Templars' financial methods and their close links with King Bela IV, as well as the Hungarian royal family's links with France and Burgundy, all add up to a strong case in favour of this hypothesis.

Hugues de Pairaud's evidence to the Inquisition in 1307 in which he said that the "idol" had four legs, two at the front and two at the back is the clearest indication of the Shroud's presence in Montpellier, then the senior priory. His assertion that he sent it there during the term of office of Pierre Allemandi places this event between 1265 and 1304. This is confirmed by the evidence of Brother Jean-Denis de Taverniac who said that Guillaume de Beaujeu, Grand Master from 1273 to 1291 was the first to hold special chapters at Voulaines at which the "idol" was exhibited.

The history of the Shroud after its appearance in Burgundy around 1356 is well attested and documented. The genealogy of its owners, Geoffrey de Charny and his wife, Jeanne de Vergy, shows that they were connected by blood and marriage to the ruling houses of Burgundy, France, England, Savoy and Hungary. The de Vergys were hereditary senseschals of Burgundy and thus responsible for carrying out the king of France's orders in that province in October 1307. Jean de Vergy, or his son, had the motive and the opportunity to take possession of the Shroud and to hide it in their kinsman's castle of Mont-Saint-Jean.

It is appropriate at this point to bring forward another scrap of circumstantial evidence which seems to fit into the pattern of events I have been describing. I have shown that in the *Great Vulgate Cycle* the Grail Castle is called Corbenic and the like, which can mean the Castle of the Blessed Body, that is to say the Castle of Corpus Christi. The Feast of Corpus Christi was unknown before 1230, and its inclusion in the Calendar of the Western Church was promulgated by Pope Urban IV in 1264. The Feast commemorates the institution and gift of the Holy Eucharist, and is observed on the Thursday after Trinity Sunday. This is the first free Thursday after Easter, the previous one being already occupied by Maundy Thursday. Its celebration is mainly due to the efforts of the Blessed Juliana of Liège (1192-1258). She was led to take action about 1230 in response to a "vision". The Archdeacon of Liège at this time was Jacques Pantaléon (ca 1190-1264), the son of a cobbler from Troyes. He was subsequently Archdeacon of Laon, and in 1249 he bought the icon, on which the artist has stated that this is the "Lord's picture on the Cloth". The icon was certainly painted in Hungary or Slavonia, and reached France by way of Southern Italy, where William de Saint-Omer had estates.

What possible reason could he have had for making such a gift if he did not believe it to be a faithful copy of the Mandylion head in Constantinople? Immediately after Pantaléon was elected Pope, he appointed Pierre de Charny, later Archbishop of Sens to be his Chamberlain. Since Pierre used the same arms as the de Charnys of Mont-Saint-Jean, there can be little doubt that he belonged to that family, although I have not been able to place him in the pedigree.

Can it be purely coincidental that Juliana's "vision" occurred at almost exactly the time when the Shroud passed into the possession of the Templars from the King of Hungary's, and that the Feast of Corpus Christi was included in the Church's calendar when the reigning Pope and his Chamberlain were from Burgundy and Champagne?

Jacques de Molay was elected Grand Master of the Order of Knights Templar at the end of 1292, eighteen months after the fall of Acre and the final expulsion of the Order from the Holy Land. The affairs of the Order at this time were consequently in some disarray. The year after his election a General Chapter was held at Montpellier under his chairmanship attended by all the senior knights. These included Pierre Allemandi, the Commander of Montpellier and Languedoc, Jean de la Tour, the Treasurer, Geoffrey de Charnay and others, including the Preceptors of Burgundy and Champagne. Immediately after the fall of Acre the Order transferred its headquarters to Cyprus, but it quickly became clear that this could only be temporary. The situation in France, however, was dominated by two factors, both dangerous to the Order. The King had recently emerged triumphant from his quarrel with Pope Boniface VIII, and as subsequent events were to prove, the Papacy no longer offered the safe shield against the greed of monarchs as it had in the past. This particular monarch was in dire need of money to enable him to carry out his centralising policy. Sooner or later the Order's immense wealth would be at risk, and although the fatal blow was not struck for another fourteen years, the Chapter would have been blind not to have seen the danger that threatened. If no decision regarding the safety of the Shroud, the Order's most treasured possession, was taken at Montpellier in 1293, it must have become increasingly apparent as the years went by that measures would have to be taken to protect it in the event of an attack by the King. The subject uppermost in the minds of the Chapter in 1293, however, was the whereabouts of the Order's headquarters should be in future now that the Holy Land had been irretrievably lost.

There were two Templar houses in Paris; one situated on the right bank of the Seine near the church of Saint-Gervais, known as the Old Temple, the other in the Faubourg du Temple outside the city walls. We know that in the end Paris was chosen, but the decision does not seem to have been easy. In June 1293 Jacques de Molay wrote to King Edward I to tell him that Guy de Foresta had been nominated Visitor of the Order in Britain, and in 1295 he went to England for Foresta's installation. It is known that serious thought was given to the possibility that the London Temple might become the Order's headquarters, and de Molay's stay in England lasted until 1300, in which year he took up residence in Paris for the first time.

In spite of dying a martyr's death, de Molay was responsible in some measure for the catastrophe which befell the Order in 1307. He was a man of limited vision, narrow-minded and obstinate. One of his contemporaries described him as "ladre" (stingy). He was never prepared to make concessions and it was a disaster to find such a mediocre man at the head of the Order at this particular juncture.

If the public accepted the Templars as true monks, the Church was hostile towards them on account of their role as bankers and managers of the royal finances. In these circumstances it would have been less than prudent to house the Shroud too close to the rapacious king. At the same time, now that the Order's centre of gravity had shifted from the Holy Land to Europe, Montpellier was no longer the geographical crossroads it had been during the Crusades. As Paris was clearly unsafe an equally accessible place had to be found for it. Voulaines in Burgundy was obviously the most convenient as it was easy to reach from all parts of France and nearer to Germany, the Low Countries and England than Montpellier.

Any decision affecting the Shroud was bound to concern the Treasurer, Jean de la Tour. He and Geoffrey de Charnay had been members of the Templar House at Étampes, but this Preceptory was too close to Paris for safety. As a Burgundian and a relative of the Seneschal, Jean de Vergy, Geoffrey must have supported the choice of Voulaines, for neither man can have overlooked the fact that both the châteaux Vergy and of Mont-Saint-Jean were only a few hours ride away.

Geoffrey de Charnay, one of the four Templars burnt at the stake in Paris in 1314, had given evidence to the Inquisition in October and November 1307. He said he was about fifty-six years old, and that he had been a member of the Order for thirty-eight years. He was admitted at Étampes by Brother Amaury de la Roche, who was Master of France in 1264. This statement places his date of birth about 1251, and his admission to the Order around 1269 or 1270. Since Geoffrey would probably have been admitted around the age of eighteen I had to find a convincing place for him in the pedigree of the de Charny family I had reconstructed. On the grounds of age he could have been the youngest son of Hugues de Charny, who I knew to have been living in 1252. If I am correct, this would make him the uncle of the first de Charny owner of the Shroud.

There is, of course, some confusion arising from the two spellings of the surname – Charny and Charnay. One source suggests that the Templar's full name was Geoffrey de Joinville de Briquenay de Charnay and that he was Marguerite de Joinville's brother. I certainly found such a brother, but his name was given as Geoffrey de Joinville de Briquenay. He was the second son of Jean de Joinville. But all the genealogical authorities I consulted said that he had been married to a wife called Marguerite and that he died without issue some time after 1294. This, of course, flatly contradicts what Geoffrey de Charnay said about himself when interrogated by the Inquisition in 1307. In the end I came to the conclusion that there were two Geoffreys, one of whom was Marguerite de Joinville's brother, and another, the Templar, who was her brother-in-law.

Forty-seven years after the catastrophe Geoffrey's nephew and namesake, and Jeanne de Vergy, his wife, at last deemed it safe to bring the Shroud to light. A generation and more had gone by, and there was no further danger from the King of France. In June 1353 King John II, the great-nephew of Philip the Fair, granted Geoffrey de Charny a rent for the foundation of his church at Lirey. Two years later he appointed this same Geoffrey Porte-Oriflamme or Standard-Bearer of France. Geoffrey was killed in September 1356 defending his sovereign at Poitiers. The previous May, his church was dedicated and the Shroud installed in it. Another year passed before it was shown to the public for the first time since it left Constantinople 150 years before.

There is, however, another account of the Shroud's "missing years", which I must now consider. In 1204, the Blachernae Palace was captured by Henry of Flanders and a troop of Burgundian soldiers. He gave orders for the relics there to be surrendered to the Bishop of Troyes, who made an inventory of them. This, as I have already pointed out, did not include any mention of the Shroud or the Mandylion. Robert de Clari states, (somewhat naively) that "some brought (the relics of the Passion) in well, others badly", so this might explain why the Shroud never came to the Bishop's notice.

According to Monsignor S.A. Barnes, Domestic Prelate to Pope Pius XI, who wrote an account of the Shroud of Turin in 1934, the relic came into the posession of Odo de la Roche, later Duke of Athens and Sparta, one of the chief Burgundian leaders. Odo sent it to his father, Ponce de la Roche, who lived in what is now known as Franche Comté, but was then the County of Upper Burgundy (Haute Bourgogne). Ponce gave it to his local diocesan, Amadeus de Tramelay, Archbishop of Besançon, for safe keeping in the cathedral, where it remained for one hundred and forty years, and where it was seen on numerous occasions. As a consequence of the Shroud's presence, Besançon became a great centre of pilgrimage.

In 1349 the cathedral of Besançon was struck by lightning, caught fire and burnt to the ground. After the fire no trace of the Shroud could be found. It had disappeared with the reliquary in which it was kept, and everyone concluded it had perished in the flames. What really happened, according to Mgr Barnes, was that one of the de Vergy family had got possession of it, and taken it to Calais, where he presented it to King Philip VI, of France. This, he supposes, was done for political reasons. Besançon was not then within the king of France's dominions, but belonged to the Empire. There was a strong party who desired that it should be annexed to France, and Mgr Barnes suggests that the de Vergy family were among these, though he admits that there is no clear proof of this, nor have I been able to find any either.

Besançon Cathedral      J. Feuillie/© C.N.M.H.S./S.P.A.D.E.M.

The king, who died in 1350, continues Mgr Barnes, entrusted the Shroud to his standard-brearer, Geoffrey de Charny, who had recently escaped from his imprisonment by the English, and it was at Amiens that the Shroud was given into his keeping. Geoffrey took it back to Champagne and kept it until he built the church at Lirey in 1356. The history of the Shroud from this time onward is unbroken, and there is no doubt that the Shroud of Turin is identical to the one at Lirey. The Bishop of Troyes, Pierre d'Arcis, it will be remembered, maintained that the Shroud of Lirey, and thus that of Turin, was only a fabrication, the work of a painter employed by Geoffrey de Charny about 1352. This theory has now been broken down completely since the Shroud of Turin has been subjected to modern examination. Consequently, a new theory has to be constructed.

According to Mgr Barnes' theory, the king of France intended Geoffrey de Charny to restore the Shroud to the Dean and Chapter of Besançon, from whom it had been stolen by his de Vergy kinsman after the fire. But Geoffrey determined to keep it for himself and fobbed off the Chapter with a copy, for which he employed an artist to paint on linen the frontal image only. This he sent to Besançon, where the Chapter accepted it as genuine.

The Canons of Lirey, conscious that they possessed the true Shroud, began to exhibit it publicly, but Henri de Poitiers, the then Bishop of Troyes, demanded that they should show proof that theirs was really what they claimed it to be. This, of course, they were unable to do, on account of the way it had come into their hands. The Bishop, believing the original had gone to Besançon consequently forbade any further exhibitions of the relic, except only as an authentic copy of the real Shroud. The Canons of Lirey had no choice but to comply. Thirty years later, during the disturbed period of the Hundred Years War, the de Charny family decided that Lirey was unsafe, and took the Shroud to Charny or Mont-Saint-Jean, where it remained until it was safe to return it to Lirey. By 1389 times were easier, and the Canons decided to exhibit it once more as the true Shroud of Christ.

This time it was Pierre d'Arcis who forbade any exhibitions, believing like his predecessor, that the true Shroud was at

Besançon. Once again, although the de Charnys and the
Canons knew that theirs was the true Shroud, they could do
nothing about it without revealing the fraud they had
perpetrated on the Besançon Chapter. For some reason no one
thought of having the two Shrouds authoritatively examined,
so the "fraud" was never discovered at that time. In 1421,
owing to renewed war with England, the danger to the Shroud
once more became acute, and the de Charny family again took
possession of it. The Besançon Shroud remained un-
questioned, though seldom exhibited, and no one examined it
closely until 1794, when it became clear that it was a painted
copy. It was then destroyed with the consent of the clergy
themselves.

In 1449, following peace with England, the Canons of Lirey
once more pressed for the return of the Shroud, but Margaret
de Charny refused to give it up, and three years later she sold
it to her kinsman, Duke Louis I of Savoy.

According to Mgr Barnes, there are two doubtful points
about this theory. He does not know for certain that the
Shroud which disappeared from Constantinople after the sack
was identical with that which was given to Besançon by Odo
de la Roche in 1208, and no one knows exactly what happened
between the fire there in 1349 and the installation of the
genuine Shroud at Lirey in 1356. Although his account of the
missing years of the Shroud and mine may at first sight appear
to be contradictory, this is not so, as I shall now explain.

The earliest clear mention of the Shroud in Constantinople
dates from 1150, where it is described by an English pilgrim as
"Sudarium quod fuit super caput ejus" (The sweat-band or
bandage which was over his head). A few years later an Ice-
landic pilgrim, Nicolas Soemundarson talks of the "Fasciae
cum sudario et sanguine Christi" (the cloths with the shroud
and blood of Christ). In 1171, William of Tyre saw the relics
during the visit of King Amaury I of Jerusalem to the Emperor
Manuel Comnenus. In 1201, Nicolas Mesarites talks about
the "burial sindons of Christ", using the word in the plural,
possibly to include the bandages round the head, and finally,
in 1204 Robert de Clari also refers to the "shrouds" in the
plural.

Now, Ian Wilson has pointed out this apparent conundrum,

for he suggests that either the Pharos chapel Mandylion or the Blachernae Sindon might have been a copy, substituted after the discovery of the full-length image was made. I have already shown that the icon of Laon, which is stated quite unequivocally to be "the portrait of the Lord on the cloth", was one of many copies of the head on the Shroud, so there is no reason to dismiss the possibility that a full length painting on linen might have been made at Constantinople or earlier (not in 1352 in France as Mgr Barnes suggests). Was what was kept in the Pharos dish the very same cloth as that exhibited at Blachernae? Was Robert de Clari told about the one in the dish but only saw with his own eyes the one at Blachernae? Whichever way one looks at it, there seems good reason for believing that there were two Shrouds in Constantinople in 1204 – the true one we see today in Turin, and a copy. We are thus free to posit that the copy found its way to Besançon through the agency of Odo de la Roche, and the genuine one found its way to France in the manner I have described in this book.

Let us look at this possibility a little more closely. Assuming that the copy Shroud reached Besançon in 1208 and survived the fire of 1349, its reputation as the genuine shroud would have been well established, for during at least half this period, if not longer, the genuine Shroud was in the Balkans or in the possession of the Templars. By the time it came into the possession of the de Charny family in 1307, it had been forgotten by most people in France. At the same time, it would have been impossible for the de Charny family to produce it as the genuine Shroud in view of the fact that they had got it illicitly from the Templars when the Order was dissolved. Thus we have a perfectly reasonable exaplanation for their otherwise unaccountable silence. No one would have believed in 1307 that the de Charny Shroud was genuine, especially in Burgundy, which is so close to Besançon, quite apart from the claims of the Cadouin Shroud in Périgord.

After the fire of 1349, however, the de Charny's might have felt justified in believing that the Besançon Shroud had been destroyed, thus opening the way for them to exhibit the genuine Shroud at Lirey, which is considerably further from Besançon than Mont-Saint-Jean. Nevertheless, when it became known that the Besançon Shroud had survived – as, indeed, it had – the de Charnys were once more placed in the same difficult position as before. Naturally, the Bishops of Troyes would have considered the Lirey Shroud to be the false one, and Mgr Barnes' explanations of what happened thereafter are thus perfectly correct. Throughout the time the Shroud belonged to the de Charny family, they were unable to prove its authenticity without revealing how they came by it. For at least a generation after the dissolution of the Order of Templars their hands were tied. When fire destroyed the cathedral of Besançon, they saw their chance to bring forth the genuine Shroud, and since the rebuilding of the cathedral took many years, we can presume that the false Shroud was kept in some safe place until such time as it could be reinstated in the church. Once this happened, the de Charny family were back where they began. I find it impossible to accept Mgr Barnes' explanation that Geoffrey de Charny palmed off a fake Shroud on the Besançon Chapter, for it is inconceivable that they would not have seen it for what it was. Thus, I cannot accept that the Besançon Shroud was ever identical with the one we know today. That it was almost certainly a Byzantine copy is quite another matter, and this theory fits the facts much better.

Sometime between 1204 and 1356 the Shroud was removed from its golden, latticework casket, the Holy Grail, which then disappeared. For generations people have thought of it solely in terms of a cup or chalice, never as a rectangular box with a latticework lid. It is therefore not beyond the bounds of reason to believe that such a casket measuring about four feet by two feet and six inches deep has survived unrecognised, and that in some public or private museum it may be lying with a label on it stating:-

CASKET: of sixth century Middle-Eastern origin.
Decoration shows Parthian influence.
Purpose unknown.

# EPILOGUE

SCIENTIFIC TESTS in the Shroud have shown that the chances against its being a forgery are now many millions to one. It is only reasonable, therefore, since at least one eminent scientist, Dr Walter McCrone, has come to doubt its authenticity, to examine my hypothesis in the light of that one chance. Dr McCrone and his colleagues submitted proposals to the Scientific Commission on the Shroud designed to answer three questions: What is the image composed of? How was it formed? Is there blood on it? Traces of iron oxide have been found on samples taken from the Shroud on sticky tape, which leads McCrone to believe that pigments of some kind were used and that consequently, the Shroud is more likely to be a forgery than not. He believes that at some time an artist has used a highly diluted reddish water-colour paint to touch up the image if not wholly to create it.

If McCrone is correct, one has to ask some further questions: How was the forgery committed? By whom might it have been committed? What was the motive of the forger, or of those who commissioned him? When was it committed? Who had the opportunity to commit it undetected?

In our present state of knowledge it is quite impossible to answer the first question, since this is the very one that has so far baffled most of the scientists who have studied the Shroud in recent years. No one has yet been able to give a naturalistic and totally convincing explanation of how the image got on to the cloth. That, of course, does not mean that it got there by supernatural means, though it has to be acknowledged that

154

that is one of several possibilities. Modern science has not yet been able to come up with a totally convincing explanation. Maybe one day it will. In the meantime the image does not seem to have been drawn or painted in a way images are usually applied to textiles. If it is a forgery, therefore, the forger must have been not only a draughtsman of outstanding genius on a level with Michelangelo, Leonardo da Vinci or Phaedias, but also strongly motivated to create such a masterpeice. When did he do it? for whom and why?

The history of the Shroud since the mid-fourteenth century is so well documented that it can be said with some certainty that the forgery must have been committed before it passed into the hands of the Duke of Savoy. In other words while it belonged to the de Charny or de Vergy families or the Templars.

There is simply no genius of this calibre known to art historians capable of creating such a masterpiece at this period. But that does not mean there was not such a genius; after all, he could have worked in total isolation and produced no other work of a comparable nature. So let us assume that he did live in some remote monastery or castle unknown to the rest of the world outside. Why did he draw Christ in this particular way – with frontal and dorsal image of the body? what could his reasons have been? Hardly for monetary gain. There is no record of the Shroud having been bought or sold before the mid-fifteenth century. If the artist had been commissioned by, let us say, Geoffrey I de Charny or by Jean or Guillaume de Joinville even by the Templars, he would surely have demanded a high price for his work. As for them, there would have been no point in commissioning such an extraordinary work unless they could see some profit from it. Even after the de Charnys exposed it to the public at Lirey, or even after it had gone to St Hippolyte-sur-Doubs, where it was seen by more people than at any other time until the twentieth century, it does not seem to have been the source of great wealth.

Many copies of it were made at that time, but none of them came close enough to the original for them to be mistaken for anything other than the work of artists who were more or less competent.

When could the Shroud have been made? Until reliable Carbon 14 or other tests have been perfected this must remain an open question, but in the light of our present knowledge the answer would seem to be during the period before it came into the hands of the de Vergy and de Charny families – that is before 1307. Once again, let us accept the existence of this thirteenth century genius and ask ourselves how this forgery might affect the hypothesis that the Holy Grail was the lattice-work casket which held the Shroud of Christ. First of all the fraudulent nature of the Shroud of Turin in no way rules out the existence of an earlier shroud, be that one genuine or false, which the Byzantines and the Crusaders knew before 1204. Of course many medieval relics were copies or out and out forgeries; no one disputes that. The Mandylion might have been one of them. That does not matter; the highly intelligent and cultured men and women who saw it in the twelfth and thirteenth centuries believed it was genuine. They also believed that the earth was flat. What is important in this context is the belief that the image of Christ enclosed within the latticework Grail was not made by human hands. They should have known the difference; there were enough repre-sentations of Christ's head in paint and mosaic for them to be able to tell. If men like Robert de Clari, Louis VII, Henry of Champagne and the thousands of others whose names we do not even know believed that the Mandylion was genuine, that, in the end, is all that matters. So far as they were concerned it was the genuine Shroud of Christ.

There is, however, a school of thought which identifies the Mandylion not with the Shroud but with the Sudarion, or towel of Veronica. This opinion is largely based upon the literal interpretation of the story of Abgar of Edessa. Could there have been two cloths bearing the miraculous image of Jesus? If there were two Crowns of Thorns there could have equally well been several cloths. But Hugues de Pairaud's evidence in 1307 seems conclusive to me. Only the Shroud could be described as a head with four legs, and only such a relic could have come from Constantinople. The changing visions of Christ described in the Grail legends correspond too closely to the special Good-Friday Masses of Byzantium to refer to a towel. They must refer to the Shroud. On the other hand, assuming there had been two similar relics, it seems to me there is just a faint possibility that the Sudarion became the Cathar treasure and not the Keramion. There were so many relics in Byzantium, and they were scattered so far and wide in 1204, it is not in the least impossible that some of them found their way into the hands of heretics.

From a linguistic point of view, de Clari's use of the word "Sydoine" rather than "sindone" is significant. This suggests to me that he was writing phonetically in French the Greek word Sudarion, which sound very much alike. It is unlikely that he saw the word written down, and even if he did, it would have been in Greek characters which he probably couldn't understand. He says quite categorically that the sydoine was the cloth in which Christ's body was wrapped; a towel could not have done that.

Whatever view we take, we must remember that those who believed in relics were not stupid ignoramuses. Even if they all were gullible fools, does that matter? In seven hundred years from now, I have no doubt that we shall be regarded in precisely the same light. What does matter is the knowledge that the Grail and its previous contents inspired many men and women to live fuller lives than they might otherwise have done. If their contemplation of it had the same effect on them as the sober reading of David Willis's factual medical account of Jesus' sufferings as revealed by the Shroud had on me, that is enough.

# CHRONOLOGY

1130 British monk, Ordericus Vitalis' account of the Mandy-lion. Geoffrey of Monmouth's History of the Kings of Britain.
1143 Philippe d'Alsace, later Count of Flanders, born.
1146 Moslems capture Edessa. St Bernard preaches Crusade.
1147 Louis VII, Eleanor of Aquitaine, Henri Count of Champagne arrive in Constantinople on Second Crusade. Spend winter there.
1148 Crusaders reach Antioch.
1149 Louis VII and Eleanor leave Holy Land, attacked by Byzantine Fleet (July), reach France autumn.
1151 Death of Abbot Suger.
1152 Divorce of Louis VII from Eleanor who marries Henry Plantagenet (Henry II of England). Henri succeeds to County of Champagne.
1154 Henry Plantagenet succeeds Stephen as King of England. Walter Map goes to Paris as a student.
1155 Henry Courtmantel born.
1157 Richard Coeur de Lion born.
1158 Geoffrey Plantagenet born.
1160 Waldensian heresy preached at Lyon.
1161 Walter Map returns to England and joins the Royal Household as a clerk.
1165 Philippe Augustus born.
1167 John Lackland born.
1175 Future Empress Mary-Margaret born. Earliest date for Chrétien's *Conte del Graal*.

1177 Chrétien's patron, Philippe Count of Flanders goes to Constantinople.
1179 Philippe of Flanders returns to France. Philippe Augustus crowned in his father's lifetime. Eleventh Ecumenical Council at Rome; Walter Map sent by Henry II, disputes with Waldensians. Pope Alexander III anathematizes Albigensians.
1180 Death of Louis VII. Median date for Chrétien's romance.
1181 Death of Henri of Champagne
1182 Walter Map begins his 'De Nugis'.
1183 Death of Henry Courtmantel. Margeurite de France marries Bela III of Hungary. Walter Map in Anjou.
1184 Frederick Barbarossa's assembly of knights at Mainz.
1185 Mary-Margaret of Hungary marries Emperor Isaac.
1186 Death of Geoffrey Plantagenet, birth of his posthumous son, Arthur of Brittany.
1188 Latest date for Chrétien's romance.
1189 Death of Henry II. Succession of Richard Coeur de Lion. Walter Map leaves Royal Household.
1190 Birth of Jacques Pantaléon at Troyes (future Pope Urban IV). Third Crusade.
1191 Death of Philippe of Flanders.
1192 Walter Map finishes 'De Nugis Curialium'. Birth of Blessed Juliana of Liège. Richard Coeur de Lion returns from Holy Land and is imprisoned.
1194 Richard Coeur de Lion returns to England and then comes to France.
1197 Walter Map appointed Archdeacon of Oxford. Innocent III elected Pope and preaches a new Crusade. Death of Geoffrey IV de Joinville.
1199 Walter Map at Angers seeking see of Hereford. Death of Richard Coeur de Lion.
1200 Earliest date for composition of *Peredur*. Latest date for first sequel of Chrétien's *Conte del Graal*. Earliest date for Wolfram's *Parzival*.
1201 Nicolas Mesarites, Keeper of the Pharos Treasury says the collection includes the Shroud. Death of Thibaud of Champagne.
1202 Death of Hugues de Vergy.

1203 Robert de Clari sees the Mandylion in Constantinople. Murder of Arthur of Brittany. Coronation of Alexis IV and Isaac co-Emperors (August).

1204 Alexius Murzuphlus organises riot against Alexius IV (January). Crusaders send deputation to Alexius IV at Blachernae (February). Deposition of Alexius IV; coronation of Murzuphlus (March). Crusaders decide to attack Constantinople. Mandylion removed from Pharos (End March).
First Crusader attack (April 6) repulsed.
Second Crusader attack (April 12). Murzuphlus and Lascaris fly.
Ex-Empress Mary-Margaret takes Mandylion (Night of April 12/13). Sack of city (April 12-15).
Boniface de Montferrat marries Ex-Empress Mary-Margaret (End April).
Baldwin of Flanders crowned Emperor (May 16).
Raymond de Pérella receives orders to repair Montségur (Autumn).
Boniface de Montferrat overruns Greece and establishes Kingdom of Thessalonica (After October).

1205 Ex-Empress Mary-Margaret in Thessalonica (takes Mandylion with her). Demetrios de Montferrat born. Foundations of Hagia Paraskevi Basilica in Thessalonica. Accession of Andrew II of Hungary.

1206 Earliest date for *Perlesvaus*. Montségur repaired. Esclarmonde de Foix takes the consolamentum. Simon de Joinville Seneschal of Champagne.

1207 Wolfram incorporates Lohengrin in *Parzival*. Death of Boniface de Montferrat. Marriage of ex-Empress Mary-Margaret to Nicholas de Saint-Omer. Innocent III excommunicates Count of Toulouse.

1208 Walter Map still alive March 15. Murder of Pierre de Castelnau Papal Legate to Toulouse (15 Jan).

1209 Public flagellation of Raymond VI of Toulouse (June 18). Crusade against Albigenses begins (July). Sack of Béziers (July 22). Fall of Carcassonne (Aug 15). Guillaume de Joinville elected Bishop of Langres. Birth of Guillaume de Saint-Omer.

1210 Walter Map dead by April 1. Latest date for *Parzival*.

1212 Latest date for *Perlesvaus*. Death of Etienne de Mont-Saint-Jean. Pons de Mont-Saint-Jean donates land to Rigny abbey. Death of Nicholas de Saint-Omer. Capture of Agen by Simon de Montfort.

1215 Simon de Montfort enters Toulouse. Earliest date for *Vulgate Cycle*. Hélinand de Froidmont mentions the Grail in his *Estoire*.

1216 Pierre de Courtenay elected Emperor of Constantinople. Death of Innocent III. Siege of Beaucaire and first defeat of Albigensian Crusaders (May-August).

1218 Death of Simon de Montfort.

1219 Guillaume I de Vergy, seneschal of Burgundy. Guillaume de Joinville appointed Archbishop of Rheims. Pierre De Montaigu, Grandmaster of the Templars.

1220 Persecution of heretics at Troyes.

1222 Death of Raymond VI of Toulouse (August). Ex-Empress Mary-Margaret leaves Thessalonica and goes to Hungary.

1223 Death of Philippe Augustus (July). Accession Louis VIII (Aug). Truce between Raymond VII of Toulouse and Amaury de Montfort (May).

1224 Amaury de Montfort leaves Languedoc (January). Jean de Joinville born (approx).

1226 Albigensian Crusade of Louis VIII (June-November). Death of Louis VIII (Nov 8). Death of Archbishop Guillaume de Joinville (Nov 6).

1229 Treaty of Meaux between French King and Albigenses. Mary-Margaret dead (approx).

1230 Median date for *Mort Artu*. Juliana of Liège promotes Corpus Christi.

1231 Montségur becomes Cathar stronghold.

1232 Guilhabert de Castres holds synod at Montségur. Death of Pierre Montaigu.

1233 Pope Gregory IX institutes the Inquisition.

1235 Latest date for the *Vulgate Cycle*. Jean de Joinville, Seneschal of Champagne (approx). Death of Andrew II of Hungary. Accession of Bela IV.

1240 Jacques Pantaléon Canon of Laon (approx). Death of Guillaume I de Vergy. Henri de Vergy becomes Seneschal of Burgundy.

1241 Tatar invasion of Hungary; defeat of Templars, Hungarian royal family retreat to Klis.
1242 Death of Guillaume de Saint-Omer at Trogir.
1243 Siege of Montségur begins (May).
1244 Fall of Montségur (March 16).
1249 Jacques Pantaléon sends Icon to Laon.
1251 Geoffrey de Charny (Templar) born (approx).
1252 Hugues de Charny gives a donation to the Abbey of Rigny.
1253 Jacques Pantaléon appointed bishop of Verdun.
1255 Jacques Pantaléon appointed Patriarch of Jerusalem.
1258 Death of Juliana of Liège.
1261 Jacques Pantaléon becomes Pope. Pierre de Charny appointed Papal Chamberlain. Jean de Joinville marries his second wife.
1267 Hugues de Pairaud admitted to the Order of Knights Templar. Pierre Allemandi appointed Preceptor of Montpellier.
1269 or 1270 Geoffrey de Charney admitted to the Order of Knights Templar.
1271 Languedoc passes to the French Crown.
1278 Jean de la Tour appointed Treasurer of the Order of Knights Templar.
1291 Fall of Acre.
1292 Jacques de Molay elected Grand Master of the Order of Knights Templar.
1293 Grand Chapter of Knights Templars held at Montpellier. Earliest possible date for the arrival of the Shroud at Montpellier.
1295 Jacques de Molay in England for inauguration of Guy de Foresta as Visitor of Britain.
1300 Geoffrey de Charny I born (approx) Jacques de Molay in Paris Temple.
1307 Jacques de Molay sees the Pope (Aug 14).
King Philippe le Bel at Abbey of Maubuisson signs order to disband the Order of Templars (Sep 23).
Jacques de Molay at funeral of Catherine de Valois (Oct 12).
Shroud removed from Voulaines to either Vergy or Mont-Saint-Jean (between Sep 25 and Oct 12).

King Philippe le Bel attacks and arrests the Templars (Oct 13).

1310  Death of Jean de Vergy, Seneschal of Burgundy.
1312  Pope Clement agrees to the dissolution of the Templars.
1318  Death of Jean de Joinville, Seneschal of Champagne.

# APPENDIX

*The Casket of the duc de Blacas*

In 1832 a carved, stone casket bearing on its lid the figure of a crowned and bearded hermaphrodite, four cabalistic symbols and an Arabic inscription came into the possession of a well-known amateur antiquarian, the duc de Blacas. It was alleged at the time that the casket had been unearthed at Essarois in 1789 on the estate of the marquis de Chastenay, some 8km south of Voulaines. The discovery caused a considerable stir in French antiquarian circles some forty years later when the duc de Blacas obtained it from an antique dealer in Dijon. It formed the subject of a lengthy monograph by Alexandre Prosper Mignard, who based upon it the theory that the Templar "heresy" had been none other than Catharism. Towards the end of the last century this casket, and another not unlike it, found their way to the British Museum, where they can still be seen on request.

Mignard was convinced that the casket was of 13th century French origin, and until I saw it, I believed that it might just have been the casket in which the Templars had kept the Shroud/Grail at Voulaines. There is, however, no possible doubt that the casket was made much later than this, probably in the eighteenth century, for it is stylistically completely unlike anything which might have been made in the 13th century. Furthermore, since it is no larger than a Georgian tea-caddy, it is quite incapable of containing anything remotely as bulky as the Shroud, or even a human head or skull.

165

It is almost certain that the casket was planted deliberately to hoodwink antiquarians into believing that the Templars were Manichaeans or Cathars, and with the probable intention of providing historical respectability for one of the secret societies, such as the Rosicrucians or Freemasons, which sprang up during and after the Revolution in France. Mignard mentions similar caskets in Germany and Austria, and his monograph, along with others written about the same time and since, probably accounts for the popular belief that these societies are direct descendants of the Templars.

# BIBLIOGRAPHY

*PART ONE*
The Holy Blood and the Holy Grail: Michael Baigent, Richard Leigh and Henry Lincoln. Cape. London 1982.
Parzival: Wolfram von Eschenbach. Trans: A.T. Hatto. Penguin Classics 1980.
The Holy Grail – Its Legends & Symbolism. A.E. Waite. London 1953.
Roman de l'Estoire dou Saint Graal: Robert de Boron.
Lewis & Shorts Latin Dictionary.
The Oxford Latin Dictionary.
Dictionnaire étymologique de la langue latine.
Glossarium Mediae et Infimae Latinitatis.
Lexicon Mediae et Infimae Latinitatis.
Dictionnaire d'ancien français: Moyen Age et Rennaissance: Larousse.
Dictionnaire étymologique de Français: Paris 1979.
The Grail from Celtic Myth to Christian Symbol: R.S. Loomis. Cardiff 1963.
A Structural Study of the 'Perlesvaus': T.E. Kelley. Droz, Geneva 1974.
Le motif du retentir dans la littérature française mediévale; des origines à 1230: J-C. Payen. Geneva 1968.
The Quest of the Holy Grail: Trans: Pauline Matarasso. Penguin Classics 1969.
Le Croisade contre le Graal: Otto Rahn. Stock, Paris, 1934, 1964, 1974.

Le Mystère d'Otto Rahn – Du Catharisme au Nazisme:
Christian Bernadac Editions France-Empire. Paris 1978.
The Death of King Arthur: James Cable. Penguin Classics
1971.
De Nugis Curialium: Walter Map. Trans T. Wright. London
1850.
The Turin Shroud: Ian Wilson. Gollancz London 1978.
The Conquest of Constantinople: Robert de Clari. Trans:
E.H. McNeal New York 1936.
Le Roman du Saint Graal. Ed. Francisque Michel: Paris
1841.

*PART TWO*
A History of the Crusades: Steven Runciman. Penguin
Classics 1954.
A History of the English-speaking People: Winston S.
Churchill.
A History of France: G.W. Kitchin. Oxford 1881.

*PART THREE*
Histoire Généalogique et Héraldique des Pairs de France: de
Courcelles. 1824.
Histoire de la Maison Royale de France: Père Anselme: Paris
1726-33.
Dictionnaire de la Noblesse: de la Chenaye-Desbois & Badier:
1844.
History of Hungary: Denis Sinor. Allen & Unwin, London
1959.
History of Hungary: Barta, Beend, Nagy and others. London
1975.
Geschichte Ungarns: L.V. Szalay. Pest 1866.
History of Hungary: Otto Zarek. London 1935.
Histoire de Dalmatie: L. Voinovitch. Paris 1934.
Geschichte der ungarischen Mittelalters: B. Homan. Berlin
1943
Les Eglises et les Monastères des grands centres byzantines:
Raymond Janin. Paris 1975.
Blue Guide to Greece: Stuart Rossiter. 1971 edition.
Description du duché de bourgogne: Courtépée.
"Dalmatia": T.G. Jackson. 1887.

## PART FOUR

Les Templiers – Ces inconnus: L. Dailliez. Librairie Academique Perrin. Paris 1980.
Histoire d'une seigneurie du Midi de la France: J. Baunel. Montpellier 1971.
Histoire générale de Languedoc: Devic et Vaissette: Ed. A. Molinier Toulouse 1885.
Les Maisons de l'Ordre du Temple dans le Languedoc Méditérranien: Emile Bonnet: Cahiers d'histoire et d'archéologie No. 50. Nîmes 1933.
Le Dossier de l'Affaire des Templiers: Lizerand. Paris 1923.
Histoire des ducs de Bourgogue de la race capetienne: E. Petit.


## PART FIVE

Le Bûcher de Montségur: Z. Oldenbourg. Gallimard, Paris 1959.
King Arthur and the Grail: Cavendish.
La Catharisme: J. Duvernoy. Privat, Toulouse. 1929.
Le Traité contre les Bogomiles de Cosmas le Prêtre: H.C. Puech & A. Vaillant. Paris 1945.
Miscellanea Giovanni Mercati V. Studi e Testi 125. Rome 1946.
Vetera Monumenta historica Hungariam sacram illustrantia: A. Theiner. Rome 1895.
Un imperatore bizantino della decadenza: Cognasso. Bessarione XXXI.
History of the Byzantine Empire: A.A. Vasiliev. 1952.
The Unholy Crusade: J. Godfrey. London 1980.
A Short History of Hungary: C.A. Macartney. Oxford 1962.
Heresies of the High Middle Ages: W.L. Wakefield & A.P. Evans. Columbia University Press 1969.
L'Influence du Bogomilisme ou les Cathares: D. Angelov. Sofia 1968.
L'Eglise dite bolgare du Catharisme occidental. Byzantinobulgarica VI. 1980.
Dualist Heresy in the Middle Ages: M. Loos. 1974.
La croisade contre les Albigeois: P. Belperron. 1961.
History of the Inquisition: H.C. Lea.
Heresy, Crusade and Inquisition in Southern France: W.L. Wakefield 1974.

The Bosnian Church, a New Interpretation: J.V.A. Fine. New
    York 1975.
Un évêque cathare: Bulletin philologique et historique 1965:
    J. Dossat. Archives Nationales, Paris 1965.

# INDEX

171

# HUNGARIAN ROYAL FAMILY 1196-1242

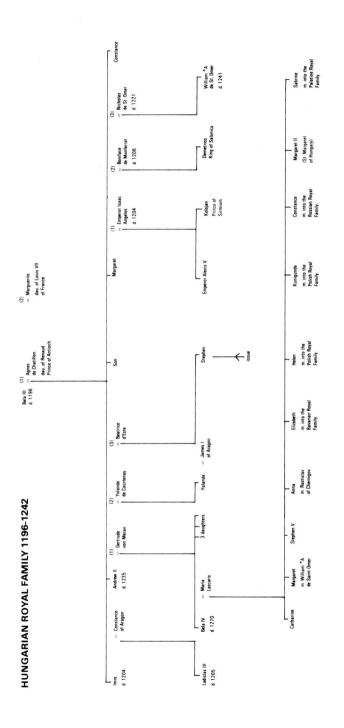